Peter Peckard

A life of Nicolas Ferrar

Peter Peckard

A life of Nicolas Ferrar

ISBN/EAN: 9783741196317

Manufactured in Europe, USA, Canada, Australia, Japa

Cover: Foto ©Andreas Hilbeck / pixelio.de

Manufactured and distributed by brebook publishing software (www.brebook.com)

Peter Peckard

A life of Nicolas Ferrar

THE LIFE OF NICOLAS FERRAR.

THESE pages contain only the private virtues of a private man; of a man endued indeed with abilities to have adorned the highest station, but of humility hardly to be found in the lowest; of a man devoting himself as it were from very infancy to the adoration of GOD, and persisting with unremitting ardour in that solemn dedication of his faculties to the last moment of his life.

Mr. Nicolas Ferrar, though not of exalted rank himself, was of a family highly respectable for that real merit which surpasses antiquity of descent or nobility of title, a family illustrious for virtue. Nor was their virtue unattended with those external claims to worldly respect, which alas! are sometimes esteemed of superior value.

Gualkeline, or Walkeline de Ferrariis, a Norman of distinction, came into England with William the

Conqueror. To Henry de Ferrariis, the second of this family, William gave Tutbury and other Castles; and more than a hundred and eighty Lordships. In process of time the family became very numerous; founded several religious houses; had the honour of peerage; and different branches of it were settled in many different counties.

Nicolas Ferrar, the father, was brought up in the profession of a merchant adventurer, and traded very extensively to the East and West Indies, and to all the celebrated seats of commerce. He lived in high repute in the city, where he joined in commercial matters with Sir Thomas and Sir Hugh Middleton, and Mr. Bateman. He was a man of liberal hospitality, but governed his house with great order. He kept a good table at which he frequently received persons of the greatest eminence, Sir John Hawkins, Sir Francis Drake, Sir Walter Raleigh, and others with whom he was an adventurer: and in all their expeditions he was ever in the highest degree attentive to the planting the Christian Religion in the New World. At home also he was a zealous friend to the Church, and always ready to supply his prince with what was required of him. He lent £300 at once upon a privy seal; a sum at that time not inconsiderable. He had the honour of being written Esquire by

Queen Elizabeth: and the exemplification of his arms is still in the family.

He married Mary Wodenoth, daughter of Laurence Wodenoth, Esquire, of the ancient family of that name, of Savington Hall, in Cheshire, where her ancestors in lineal descent had enjoyed that lordship near five hundred years, and were allied to the principal families of that county.

Mary Wodenoth was surpassed by none in comeliness of body or excellence of beauty. She was of modest and sober deportment, and of great prudence. Of few words, yet when she spoke, Bishop Lindsell was used to say of her, he knew no woman superior to her in eloquence, true judgment, or wisdom: and that few were equal to her in charity towards man, or piety towards GOD.

This worthy couple lived together many years in harmony and happiness, perfecting their holiness in the fear of GOD, and in the conscientious practice of every duty. They saw descended from them a numerous, and a virtuous family, of whose education they took uncommon care. They did not spoil their children by absolutely sparing the rod, but what occasional severity they judged to be necessary was so softened by tenderness and affection, as to produce not only the fear of doing amiss, but the love of doing well. And certainly the same method would even in the present age produce beneficial, or prevent pernicious, effects. When moral discipline, as in these our days, is neglected, we have reason to look forward to the worst consequences. And when reprehension is joined with austerity it always fails of its pretended purpose; but when it plainly appears to proceed from affection, there is scarce a disposition to be found so obstinate that it will not soon become tractable. The little instances of corrective discipline exercised by these affectionate parents, in the beginning of the seventeenth century, would perhaps excite the derision of the fastidious reader; they are therefore omitted. Nevertheless they were well calculated to impress the tender mind with a reverential awe for the Supreme Being; with obedience to parents and instructors; with universal and disinterested benevolence; with modesty, with humility, and a proper sense of subordination; with an abhorrence of all vice, but particularly of every species of falsehood. Thus did their censures tend to form and produce virtuous and valuable citizens.

The children were all constantly trained in virtue and religion. Their daily practice was to read, and to speak by memory some portion of the Scriptures, and parts of the lives of the martyrs: they were also made acquainted with such passages of history as were suited to their tender years. They were all instructed in music; in performing on the organ, viol, and lute, and in the theory and practice of singing; in the learned and modern languages; in curious needleworks, and all the accomplishments of that time. The young men, when arrived at years of discretion, had permission each to choose his profession, and then no expense was spared to bring him to a distinguished excellence in it. For this was an invariable maxim with the parents, that having laid a firm foundation in religion and virtue, they would rather give them a good education without wealth, than wealth without a good education.

The parish church and chancel of S. Bennet Sherhog in London, Mr. Ferrar repaired and decently seated at his own expense; and as there was not any morning preacher there, he brought from the country Mr. Francis White, and made him their first lecturer. Mr. White was afterwards advanced to the See of Ely.

When a stranger preached, Mr. Ferrar always invited him to dinner, and if it was discovered that he was in any necessity, he never departed without a handsome present. In truth they never were without a clergyman as a companion in their house, or even on their journeys, as they always accustomed themselves to morning and evening prayer.

Nicolas Ferrar, the third son of this worthy couple, was born the 22nd, and christened the 23rd, of February, 1592, in the parish of S. Mary Stayning in Mark Lane, London. His godfathers do not appear. His godmother was a Mrs. Riggs, wife to Captain Riggs, who recommended herself highly to the esteem of Queen Elizabeth, by an heroic act which she performed upon the seashore at Dover, in 1588.

He was a beautiful child of a fair complexion, and light coloured hair. At four years of age he was sent to school, being of a tractable disposition and lively parts. At five he could read perfectly, or repeat with propriety and grace a chapter in the Bible, which the parents made the daily exercise of their children. By the brightness of his parts, and the uncommon strength of his memory, he attained with great ease and quickness whatsoever he set himself to learn; yet was he also remarkably studious; being a rare instance of the union of the brightest parts with the most intense industry. He was particularly fond of all historical relations, and when engaged in this sort of reading, the day did not satisfy him, but he would borrow from the night; insomuch that his mother would frequently seek him out, and force him to partake of some proper recreation. Hence, even in his childhood, his mind was so furnished with historical anecdotes, that he could at any time draw off his schoolfellows from their play, who would eagerly surround him, and with the utmost attention listen to his little tales, always calculated to inspire them with a love of piety and goodness, and excite in them a virtuous imitation.

When he was very young he was entered into Latin at London, at the desire of his master, though others thought it too soon: but he was so eager and diligent in his application that he soon surpassed all his companions.

He was of a grave disposition, and very early showed a great dislike of everything that savoured of worldly vanity. In his apparel he wished to be neat, but refused all that was not simple and plain. When bands were making for the children, he earnestly entreated his mother that his might not have any lace upon them, like those of his brothers, but be made little and plain, like those of Mr. Wotton, "for I wish to be a preacher as he is." Mr. Wotton was a learned Divine, and reader of Divinity in Gresham College. He was frequently at Mr. Ferrar's, and always examined and exercised young Nicolas, being wonderfully delighted with his ingenuity.

He was good-natured and tender-hearted to the

highest degree; so fearful of offending any one, that upon the least apprehension of having given displeasure, he would suddenly weep in the most submissive manner, and appear extremely sorry. His temper was lovely, his countenance pleasing: his constitution was not robust, but he was active, lively, and cheerful. Whatsoever he went about he did it with great spirit, and with a diligence and discretion above his years.

And now the parents were informed by their friends, and by Mr. Francis his schoolmaster, that it was time to send him to some greater school where he might have a better opportunity to improve himself in the Latin tongue. It was thereupon resolved to send him and his brother William to Enborn, near Newbury in Berkshire, to the house of Mr. Brooks, an old friend, who had many other pupils, who was a religious and good man, but a strict disciplinarian.

While preparations were making for this journey, an event took place which made the deepest and most lively impression upon the mind of young Nicolas, and strongly marks his character, and the bent of his disposition. He was but six years of age, and being one night unable to sleep, a fit of scepticism seized his mind, and gave him the greatest perplexity and uneasiness. He doubted whether there was a GOD? and if there was, what was the most acceptable mode of serving Him? In extreme grief he rose at midnight, cold and frosty, and went down to a grass plat in the garden, where he stood long time sad and pensive, musing, and thinking seriously upon the great doubt which thus extremely perplexed him. At length throwing himself on his face upon the ground, and spreading out his hands, he cried aloud, "Yes, there is, there must be a GOD: and He, no question, if I duly and earnestly seek it of Him, will teach me not only how to know, but how to serve Him acceptably. He will be with me all my life here, and at the end will hereafter make me happy."

These are exalted and wonderful sentiments for a child of six years old: and this anecdote may influence the reader to give credit to those sublime ecstasies of devotion which he experienced and expressed at the close of his life.

His doubts now vanished, his mind became easy, and he returned to his apartment: but the remembrance of what he felt on this occasion made him ever after strongly commiserate all who laboured under any religious doubt, or despair of mind. And in the future course of his life he had repeated opportunities to exert his benevolence to those who experienced a similar unhappiness.

In the year 1598, he was sent to Enborn School, near Newbury in Berkshire, where he made such a rapid progress in Latin, Greek, and logic, that he soon became the first scholar of his years. He strengthened his memory by daily exercise: he was a great proficient in writing and arithmetic, and attained such excellence in short-hand, as to be able to take accurately a sermon or speech on any occasion. He was also well skilled both in the theory and practice of vocal and instrumental music.

Thus accomplished, in his fourteenth year, his master, Mr. Brooks, prevailed with his parents to send him to Cambridge, whither he himself attended him, and admitted him of Clare Hall, presenting him, with due commendation of his uncommon abilities to Mr. Augustin Lindsell, the tutor, and Dr. William Smith, then master of the college.

His parents thought proper, notwithstanding the remonstrance of some friends against it, to admit him a Pensioner for the first year; as they conceived it more for his good, to rise by merit gradually to honour. In this situation, by excellent demeanour, and diligent application to his studies, he so deported himself in all things, and to all persons, that he instantly gained the affections and applause of all who knew him, performing all his exercises with distinguished approbation.

NICOLAS FERRAR. 11

Mr. Lindsell spared not to make full proof of his abilities, wishing, as he was used to express himself, to see his inside, as well as his outside. He therefore made many trials of his abilities, which the rest of the Fellows thought unreasonable; saying "it was a shame to spur a fleet horse, which already outwent the rider's own desire, and won every race he put him to." When they urged that he required impossibilities, he would reply, "Content yourselves a little, you shall see what the boy can do, and that too without much trouble." These proofs of wonderful abilities were continually repeated, and he thus went on from day to day improving in all good learning. His attention and diligence was such, that it was observed, his chamber might be known by the candle that was last put out at night, and the first lighted in the morning. Nor was he less diligent in his attendance at chapel, than at his studies, so that his piety and learning went on hand in hand together.

In his second year he became Fellow-commoner, and being now every day more and more the companion of the Fellows, he every day became more and more esteemed by them. In 1610 he took his degree of Bachelor of Arts. At this time he was appointed to make the speech on the King's Coronation Day (July 25), in the College

Hall; and the same year he was elected Fellow of that Society.

If we take a view of him at this period when he became Fellow, we shall find that his natural parts were wonderfully improved, his memory so enlarged and strengthened, that he had read nothing of worth, but he had made it his own, and could always instantly apply it to the present occasion. He spoke also and wrote, and argued with such ingenious dexterity that very few indeed were equal to him. Nevertheless he was still so eager in the pursuit of farther acquisitions, that industry and genius seemed to be incorporated in him. Nor was he more attentive to his own instruction, than to the happiness of all with whom he was concerned. For he was a constant and indefatigable promoter of peace; and when any difference had arisen, he had the art so to win upon each side, that he would draw the contending parties from their unfriendly resolutions, and reanimate and establish harmony between them. Mr. Lindsell was used to say of him, "May GOD keep him in a right mind! for if he should turn schismatic or heretic, he would make work for all the world. Such a head, such power of argument! such a tongue, and such a pen! such a memory withal he hath, with such indefatigable pains, that, all these joined together,

I know not who would be able to contend with him."

His constitution was of feminine delicacy, and he was very subject to aguish disorders; yet he bore them out in a great measure by his temperance, and by a peculiar courageousness of spirit which was natural to him. His favourite sister, married to Mr. Collet, lived at Bourne Bridge, near Cambridge. And as the air of Cambridge was found not well to agree with him, he made frequent excursions to Bourne Bridge, where he passed his time in the pursuit of his studies, and in the instruction of his sister's children.

But his tutor, Mr. Lindsell, and others of the Fellows, having now apprehension of his health, carried him to Dr. Butler, the celebrated Physician, of Cambridge, who had been of Clare Hall, and was a particular friend of Mr. Lindsell. Dr. Butler conceived a great affection for Mr. Ferrar, and exerted all his skill; yet still the disorder increased more and more upon him; and at length this good Physician said, "Why should I give thee any more prescriptions? all I can do will not conquer this distemper. Alas! all I can say is, you must henceforth deal with this disorder when it comes to you, as men do with beggars, when they have a mind to disuse them from their houses, give them nothing but let them go as they came. You must through a spare diet, and great temperance even all your life long, seek to be quit of this unhappy companion: he must be starved away."

For some time after this Mr. Ferrar grew better, but soon relapsed again, and in the autumn of 1612 he began to grow very ill. His friends now feared he would not get over the winter. Dr. Butler said, "I can do no more for him, the last remedy or hope I can give you is from the change of air. He must go in the spring to travel. I doubt not but I can keep him up this winter, and if travel recover him not, nothing will. Besides, it is high time his mind be taken off from these his incessant studies; these alone, if he be permitted to go on, will speedily destroy his constitution. The course I propose may prolong his life till he is thirty-five years of age; but longer in my judgment it will not last. In the mean time he will live to do great good. And think not that his time spent in travel will be lost; no: depend upon it he will improve himself greatly. Mr. Lindsell, go your way; think of it: persuade his parents to it. I can say no more to you. Let him go next spring. I will take care of him this winter." And so he did most affectionately.

Mr. Ferrar was now almost seven years standing in the University, and was to take his Master of

Arts degree at the ensuing Midsummer, 1613; and he had already performed with great credit all his previous exercises.

It being made known to the Heads of the University that he was to travel, and to have the opportunity of going with that noble company which then went with the Lady Elizabeth to conduct her to the Palatinate with the Palsgrave her husband, it was propounded that he might have the favour of cap and hood immediately, though before the usual time, so as to be complete Master of Arts, before his departure, which was readily granted, and immediately his Graces were given him. And now many came to present their most affectionate wishes to him for health and happiness in his travels. And thus he bade Cambridge adieu.

Being come to the end of Mr. Ferrar's Academical life, I will here insert a Letter from Dr. Byng, a cotemporary in the same society, as a collateral testimony of his uncommon abilities and exemplary conduct during the whole time of his Collegiate education.

"Dr. Rob. Byng to Mr. Barnabas Oley.

"Sir,

"Concerning the request in your second letter, I wish I was as able as I am willing to deliver the choicest virtues of our dear and worthy friend Mr. N. Ferrar unto posterity: whom as I truly loved whilst he lived, so I am one that shall ever honour his blessed memory.

"As for the time of his admission into our College of Clare Hall, he was, as I did then guess by his stature and dimensions, about thirteen years of age, when yet his deportment was such as spake him more a man than many are at four and twenty: there was so sweet a mixture in him of gravity with affability, and modesty with civility.

"After the commendable performances of his acts in the Schools, it pleased the University to grace him with the degree of Bachelor of Arts. And his worth was so well known in the College, that he was selected to make the oration upon the Coronation day, which he performed with great applause. And the then Master of the College, Dr. Smith, was thereupon so taken with him, that he was pleased to ask a near friend of his 'whether the young gentleman did intend to continue in the life of a Scholar.' And receiving answer, that it was his settled resolution, he was not nice to express his good opinion of him to be such as he thought him well worthy to be elected into our Society. Wherein he showed himself to be most real, by making choice of him at the very next election, with the unanimous consent of all the co-electors then present at the meeting for that purpose.

"From that time to the taking of his next degree he was a constant resident with us in our College; during which space his comportment was such in all respects, as that it was exemplary not only to his inferiors and equals, but to many who were much his ancients, who were all so much pleased with his company, as that they thought themselves happiest, who most enjoyed it.

"As he was ever a most constant student, so none more careful to give his attendance on the College Chapel at times of Prayer. . . .

Before completing his degree of M.A. he began his travels into foreign parts. Where, how long he continued, his brother Mr. John Ferrar can best inform you. But so well did he improve the time that he spent therein, as that beside the knowledge which he had gained in the principal of the Western languages, Low and High Dutch, Italian, French and Spanish, he had thoroughly mastered the history of all places where he had resided: as myself, with many others who had the happiness to hear him discourse thereof, can give due testimony.

"From the time of his return unto the College, as he continued ever an indefatigable Student, so he was an extraordinary proficient, as having attained within a few years unto that degree of knowledge in Divinity, that he did not only overtake, but get the start of many who were much his ancients, and such as were worthily held in reputation for their great learning by the ablest Divines both in the College and the University. This was the less to be wondered at in our worthy friend, because as he was of a very sharp wit, and most clear comprehension, so also of a most solid judgment, and retentive memory; by means whereof he could fully explain the view of any author he had gone through, as myself can testify amongst other of his contemporaries. In this respect as he had not many equals, so he had few who could compare with him for his exact skill in the Book of Books, the Holy Scriptures; which he made from his cradle, as I may say, so familiar to him by his daily and diligent reading, and meditating thereon, as that he was able to turn readily to any place without the help of a Concordance.

"Certainly, Sir, to give him his due commendation, I may truly say that he was Homo perpaucorum hominum, et ad omnia natus.[1]

"In all which respects as he was eminent whilst he resided in the University, so he gave full demonstration thereof to his dearest and nearest friends at Little Gidding, where in his last and best

[1] A man of ten thousand and had a genius for everything.

times he was a burning and a shining Light. And therefore I advise the writer of his Life to repair to such of his friends as are there yet living, who are able to furnish him with such store of choice materials, and so exactly squared unto his hands that they will fit into the goodly structure which he is now erecting for the preservation of his precious memory here on earth, who now shines more gloriously among the ever-blessed Saints in the highest heavens. Tuus ex animo.[1]

"ROBERTUS BYNG.

"Ashlington, Com. Wilts,
Idibus Septembris,[2] 1654.

"To his much respected friend Mr. Oley, at Mr. Garthwaites, Stationer, at the North door of S. Paul's. These present."

All things being settled with respect to his going abroad, Mr. Ferrar left the following written Farewell to his family, which his mother found in his study a few days after he was gone.

"Since there is nothing more certain than Death, nor more uncertain than the time when; I have thought it the first and chiefest wisdom for a man to prepare himself for that which must one day come, and always be ready for that which may every hour happen: especially considering how

[1] Sincerely yours.   [2] Sept. 13.

dangerous any error is here, which cannot be amended: neither is any one the nearer to Death for having prepared for it. It is then a thing of exceeding madness and folly to be negligent in so weighty a matter, in respect whereof all other things are trifles. I here confess my own wretchedness and folly in this, that through the common hope of youth, I have set death far from me: and persuading myself that I had a long way to go, have walked more carelessly than I ought. The good LORD GOD be merciful unto me.

"Indeed I have a long way to run, if death stood still at the end of threescore years: but GOD knows if he be not running against me, if he be not ready to grasp me, especially considering the many dangers wherein I am now to hazard myself, in every one whereof death dwells. If GOD be merciful to me, and bring me safe home again, I will all the days of my life serve Him in His Tabernacle, and in His Holy Sanctuary.

"I hope He who hath begun this mind in me will continue it, and make me to walk so as I may be always ready for Him, when He shall come either in the public Judgment of all the world, or in private Judgment to me by death. This is my purpose and this shall be my labour.

"And you, my most dear Parents, if GOD shall

take me from you, I beseech you be of good comfort, and be not grieved at my death, which I undoubtedly hope shall be to me the beginning of eternal happiness. It was GOD that gave me to you, and if He take me from you, be not only content but joyful that I am delivered from the vale of misery. This GOD that hath kept me ever since I was born, will preserve me to the end, and will give me grace to live in His Faith, to die in His Favour, to rest in His Peace, to rise in His Power, and to reign in His Glory.

"I know, my most dear parents, your tender affections towards your children, and fear your grief if GOD take me away. I therefore write and leave this, that you might know your son's estate, and assure yourselves that though he be dead to you, yet he is alive to GOD.

"I now most humbly beseech you to pardon me in whatsoever I may have at any time displeased you: and I pray GOD to bless and keep you: to give you a happy life here, and everlasting in the world to come.

"Your most humble and obedient Son,
"N. FERRAR.

" Postscript:
"My dearest Brothers and Sisters: If I live you shall find me a faithful and loving brother unto you

all: if I die, I beseech you by the fear of GOD, by the duty to your Parents, by the bond of nature, by the love you bear me, that you all agree in perfect love and amity; and account every one the other's burthen to be his; so may plenty and prosperity dwell among you. So prays your faithful and loving brother,

"N. FERRAR.

"If I die, I desire that the value of £5 of my books may be given to the College: the rest I leave to my Father's and Mother's disposing: yet I desire that in them my worthy Tutor Lindsell and Cousin Theophilus may be remembered: and if any of my sister's sons prove a scholar, the rest may be given to him.

"This 10th day of April, being Sunday."

CHAPTER II.

HIS Parents' consent and the College licence obtained, and the favour of the University granted with respect to his degree, Mr. Ferrar prepared to set out upon his travels; a course of life undertaken upon Dr. Butler's counsel for the restoration of his health, and to take him off from his incessant application to his studies. He also himself had a desire to see foreign countries for the farther acquisition of knowledge. And as he well understood the grounds of his Religion, and was convinced of its truth on Scriptural authority, as he had read most of the Fathers, and controversial writings between the Church of England and the Church of Rome, and as he had a memory so retentive, that he forgot nothing which he had read, but was able at all times to bring it forth, and apply it to the present occasion, being thus armed beforehand against whatever might occur, and relying wholly upon the mercy of GOD to protect him, with the most virtuous resolutions of heart he set out upon his travels.

His Tutor Lindsell solemnly protested that had he not perfectly known his wonderful abilities and uncommon virtue, he should not in these so tender years of his pupil have been a promoter of his travelling in the manner he did alone; but would have provided some worthy tutor to attend him. He knew that in all virtue Nicolas Ferrar was an old man, so firmly fixed in his religious principles that there was no fear of his being seduced by anything that he should hear or see. He knew that the stock of learning, wisdom and religion which he carried out with him, would be increased at his return.

With these encouragements did Mr. Lindsell appease the fears and tender anxieties of his parents at parting with him: for they bade him farewell under the dread of never seeing him again. And indeed not without reason: for he was then far from being recovered of his aguish disorder: but Dr. Butler said the sea would remove it, and they would soon hear that he was freed from his infirmity.

Some time before this, Dr. Scot, the King's sub-almoner, was made Master of Clare Hall, in the place of Dr. Smith removed to be Provost of King's. He conceived a high respect and affection for Nicolas Ferrar, and undertook that he should be introduced to the Lady Elizabeth, to go in her company and retinue; she being now ready to depart with the Prince Palsgrave her husband, who were to go first to Zealand, then to Holland, and from thence home to the Palatinate. Dr. Scot therefore took Mr. Ferrar to Court, to kiss her Royal Highness' hand: not now in the garb of a Scholar, but habited as one of the Gentlemen who belonged to her. As for him he took no delight in these gay garments, but submitted from a sense of propriety to be thus clad, and to satisfy his friends more than himself. Dr. Scot also introduced him, and procured him the knowledge and acquaintance of the whole attendance with the English Courtiers who then went with the Lady Elizabeth. Being now provided with his bills of exchange, he went in the same ship with the Master of the Green Cloth, who took an especial liking to him. They arrived happily at Flushing, where the Royal Fleet landed their passengers. And in this voyage Mr. Ferrar found the benefit of the sea air, which as Dr. Butler told him it would, cleared him of all the remains of his disorder. At Middleburgh the Lady Elizabeth was highly entertained and feasted with all her noble attendants; and Mr. Ferrar as one of her Gentlemen wanted for no marks of due notice and respect. Here he made strict observation of everything worth seeing, and gained a sufficient acquaintance with the language to serve him for all ordinary affairs and occasions. From thence the Lady Elizabeth passed on from city to city, in all which she was received with great honour, and came to the Hague: from thence to Amsterdam, where she was more magnificently entertained than at any former place. In all these towns Mr. Ferrar visited the several meeting houses of the Brownists, Anabaptists, and other Protestant Dissenters, both to observe their manners and teaching, and to see if all were answerable to his own former reading. At all which times he noted their errors, and greatly confirmed himself in his own opinions. The Jewish Synagogue likewise he left not unseen, and their orders. But that which chiefly attracted his notice at Amsterdam was their Guest, or Almshouses, where young children of both sexes are brought up to learn handicrafts. Here he got particular information of all their proceedings, and very liberally rewarded the attendants. He particularly admired the stateliness, and neatness of the Dutch in these public edifices, and the wonderful good orders and rules by which they are governed. He also visited their churches, heard their sermons, and attended all their religious rites and ceremonies. He next observed their magazines for all sorts of stores : innumerable boats and ships, and noted the different way of building from ours in the structure of their war ships. Ours he perceived were stronger made, but theirs formed with more advantage for speedy sailing. He was also charmed with their cleanliness and the many good orders everywhere observed to that intent. And he observed that the whole nation kept their houses elegantly neat in all places. When he came to his lodgings he regularly entered all his observations in a book which he kept for that purpose.

NICOLAS FERRAR. 27

The Princess Royal now directed her course towards the Palatinate, which was different from the route intended by Mr. Ferrar, who had resolved to pass through the lower parts of Westphalia, and so to Bremen, Staad, Hamburgh, Lunenburgh, Lubeck, Leipsic, and so on to the upper parts of Germany. This his determination he made known to the Lady Elizabeth's chief attendants, who warmly pressed him to accompany them to Heidelburg, the Palsgrave's Court, and chief city of the Palatinate. They told him that her Highness had taken such good notice of him herself, and had heard so much of him from the commendations of others, that if he sought preferment by his travels, he might now, even at the first, make a very fair step towards it. There was no doubt but he might be made her Secretary, that she would think him well worthy of that place and might recommend him to a better. He humbly thanked them for their good opinion, but assured them they were mistaken in his abilities. He was then introduced to her Royal Highness, and kissed her hand, who bade him farewell, and wished him much happiness in his travels.

Mr. Ferrar now set forward on his journey from Amsterdam to Hamburgh, and on his way thither he travelled for some time with a person for his guide, who had but one eye. After some days' travel they passed by a wood, where was a gibbet and some bodies hanging in chains. Now, said the postman, Sir, look yonder, those villains there hanging some years since set upon my waggon, wherein were an English youth and a Hamburgh merchant, then newly come out of Spain. The rogues carried us into that wood in a cold frosty morning and stripped us: and they found good gold tied up in the shirts of the gentlemen who had travelled with me, which they took, then drank up our wine, and went away laughing. But some time after, they, still using the same trade, set upon another waggon, whose passengers made some resistance, when they shot three of them dead in the waggon, and then fled. They were afterwards taken and there hanged as you see. Your history is true, said Mr. Ferrar, for that English youth was my brother. He has told me this story himself. And when I first saw you, I knew you to be the postman with whom he travelled, for he described you as having but one eye.

At length he arrived at Hamburgh, where the Factors of the Merchant Adventurers were resident, to whom his father and brother were well known. Here he found fresh bills of exchange, and letters from his father to Mr. Gore, his old acquaintance, and then deputy Governor of the Company; who received Mr. Ferrar with great friendship and respect, and provided a convenient lodging for him. During his stay here he procured a Scholar of the country to attend him daily at his lodgings, and instruct him in the High Dutch language, in which he made such a proficiency as to be of great service in the course of his travels. Here also in the afternoon he spent some hours in examining the curiosities in this city, and in the places adjacent. And here he informed himself by reading the histories in the Dutch language, and by discourse with men of learning in the place, of the original of this and the neighbouring cities; of their several sorts of government; their religion; ecclesiastical establishment; their trades; their commerce; the nature and disposition of the people, and their particular virtues and vices.

From Hamburgh Mr. Ferrar travelled up the country through many cities, at each of which he stayed a sufficient time to see, and make observations upon all things worthy of notice, which he regularly entered into his book for that use in short-hand.

In this manner he passed up to the University of Leipsic in Saxony: where, having proper letters of credit, he resolved to abide for some time, both to perfect himself in the High Dutch language, and to gain also what other knowledge and learning he could in that place; and to acquaint himself with the manner of ordering all things in that University. He lodged himself therefore in a principal house of that city, which by a friend's help he obtained permission to do; and the people there were very civil and courteous to him. The English factors showed him much respect, and were greatly delighted with his pleasant disposition and temper. And they were the more taken with him when they saw that he would not upon any terms drink wine or any strong drink, and had also observed his great temperance in all things, and that he was very humble and meek in his behaviour. Yet still they saw him gallant and rich in apparel. But that fashion of dress his parents thought was the best for him to make use of in his travels, that so, according to the mode of the world, he might have the easier admittance into all places, and all respectable company.

At Leipsic he made inquiry after all the ablest Scholars in every art and science in that University, who could be procured for money to teach him; and he paid them all most liberally, and far beyond their expectations. From these circumstances he was thought to be some person of great account. These his several tutors coming to him at set times, and on several days, and his personal resorting with the utmost diligence to all the exercises performed in the public schools, made him to be very much noticed. He gained great reputation for his uncommon abilities, his diligence, and his sweet deportment; his extraordinary quickness in attaining whatsoever he set himself to, the elegant Latin which he spake with the utmost readiness, and his abundant knowledge in several sorts of learning. The universal admiration he obtained was also much heightened by his being so very young. His acquaintance was desired by all the learned men of that University: and he being free in all courtesy to enter into discourse with them, many every day resorted to him. But finding that this took up too much of his time, he privately retired into lodgings in a village in the neighbourhood, and there enjoyed a better opportunity to follow the studies he had resolved upon; his tutors attending him there as they had done before. And here he passed some time in reading over the best authors who had written on the German nation, and in acquainting himself with the nature of their government, laws, and customs.

The connection of the English factors at Leipsic with their principals at home, soon transmitted the fame of Nicolas Ferrar to England, who was deemed and represented as a person who had some great intent in his mind, but that it was feared by all that he could not live to be a man of any considerable years.

As on one hand his parents could not but rejoice on hearing these accounts, so on the other they could not help fearing that his extreme application might, though at present he was in perfect health, nevertheless decay his strength, and shorten his life. They therefore exhorted him to curb his too diligent mind, and to abate of his incessant studies, for that they would allow him what time and money he would for his expenses.

Having now learned what he could at Leipsic, he departed from thence for Prague, and there he abode a considerable time, till he was able to converse fluently in the High Dutch language. From thence he wandered up and down, to every great place here and there, sometimes backwards, sometimes forwards, visiting Augsburg, Strasburg, Nuremburg, Ulm, Spires, the Emperor's Court, and so from one Prince's Court to another, observing everywhere their manner of living, and spending their time; what magazines of arms they had; what retinues they kept; what their incomes were; from whence they had their origin; what had been their revolutions; and accurately noting down whatever Germany had in any place worth recording. There being also in several parts of Germany very ingenious handicrafts of various sorts, in all these he acquired a considerable degree of knowledge. So that there was scarce any trade, art, skill or science concerning which he could not discourse to the astonishment even of the professors themselves in their respective professions. He was master also of the technical terms of their several mysteries, and could speak properly to them in their own dialect. He could express all those things that belong to war, soldiery, and arms, all that belong to ships, and navigation, and was perfect in all the mariners' peculiar phrases, and in all the particularities of every trade and occupation in common life. And in truth all this without any great care or trouble. For his penetration was so acute, and his memory so vast, and retentive; that everything he read, or heard, or saw was all his own, and he could instantly apply it to the occasion that presented itself, as all who knew him found by daily proof.

From Germany, Nicolas Ferrar bent his course for Italy. But the plague being at that time in many towns of Germany, when he came into the Venetian territories, he was obliged to remain thirty days in one place in a lazaretto, where he was shut up for public security; but was allowed a chamber to himself. Here he had leisure to recollect all those things, which to that time had passed in his travels; to review his notes and observations, which he had before all along put into short-hand; and to digest them into better order for his future use. Here also he had time to meditate what he was to do in Italy; how to order himself and his future life to the best advantage to attain his several ends in travel. Having completed the thirty days of his confinement, and being again at liberty to prosecute his journey, it may not be amiss to relate a remarkable escape he had upon the road between Prague and Padua. As he rode one day upon some very narrow and dangerous passages of the Alps, his guide being somewhat before him, suddenly from the side of a hill came an ass laden with a great piece of timber. The passage down the hill was extremely narrow, on one side very high and precipitous above him, and on the other also precipitously steep and fearful, so that if any man fell, nothing but immediate death could be expected. The timber did not lie, as at first laid on, lengthwise, but quite across the ass's back, and reached the whole breadth of the pass from one side to the other, and the beast came down the hill apace. The guide who was advanced a few yards, and had passed the narrow crevice through which the ass came into the common road, seeing Mr. Ferrar's situation, cried out in terror. The man's exclamation caused Mr. Ferrar to look up, who was carefully regarding his horse's steps, and was then upon the extreme brink of the precipice. There was but a moment between him and certain destruction; when in that moment, just as the beast came upon him she tripped, and by that motion the timber was turned the right way as it was at first laid on. Mr. Ferrar then suddenly stopping his horse upon the very edge of the precipice, there stood still, till, as it pleased GOD, the beast went quietly on with her burthen, and passed him without any harm but a slight stroke from the timber. After this providential escape, for which he returned his most devout thanks to GOD, he proceeded on his road to Padua, and so on to Venice without any other disaster.

Having stayed a convenient time at Venice, where he enjoyed the advantage of frequent access to the house and table of the English Ambassador, to whom he bore letters of introduction, he returned to Padua, which before he had only passed through, but now resolved to settle there for some time; in order to perfect himself in all the learning and knowledge to be attained in that University. Here therefore he procured tutors in those sciences in which he intended to be farther instructed. And he won their highest admiration at his ingenious questions and answers, his ready apprehension, his earnest prosecution, and his wonderful proficiency, in so many and such various studies, which at the same time seemed to him no other than so many several recreations. His acquaintance was courted by all the learned men in the University, but particularly by the most eminent Physicians; as he bestowed uncommon diligence in the pursuit of medical knowledge. And this he did from a double motive, both because he held the Physic Fellowship at Clare Hall, and also on account of the infirm, and precarious state of his own health: in which respect a proper proficiency in the science of medicine might be peculiarly serviceable to him. And now his friendship with the Paduan Physicians, and their high esteem and great love for him, was of singular benefit to him: for he fell very dangerously ill of a disorder which in all human probability would have proved fatal, had it not been for their watchful care, and most tender attentions.

It has been suggested[1] that upon his recovery from this illness, he made a vow of perpetual celibacy: and that he would upon his return to England, as soon as he could conveniently, settle his affairs for that purpose, and endeavour to spend

[1] Postscript to Herbert's Country Parson: A preparatory View, &c.

the remainder of his life in a religious retirement. But this is very uncertain; yet, if it be true it will account for a very remarkable instance of self-denial, which will occur in the future part of his life.

While Mr. Ferrar continued thus at Padua, to establish his health, and pursue his studies, he had an opportunity of exercising his great faculty in quieting a troubled mind. For now an English gentleman of the name of Garton came thither, who by the impious custom of duelling had killed another, and had fled from his country to avoid the punishment which the laws adjudge to murderers. He was under the deepest melancholy, but concealed the cause of his uneasiness. At length however he acquainted Mr. Ferrar with his misfortune, declaring his great contrition, and sincere repentance; and beseeching him to give him counsel and comfort. Mr. Ferrar by his spiritual consolations, his persuasive arguments, and wonderful power over the human mind, at length made the unhappy sufferer more easy and composed, and confirmed him in the hope of forgiveness. And this event laid the foundation of a sincere and most affectionate friendship between them.

Mr. Ferrar thus passing his time between Venice and Padua in a course of learning and virtue, and in the most laudable pursuits, he was much sought after, and visited by the English who were then also on their travels; who were delighted with his conversation, notwithstanding that his way of life and manner of thinking were very different from their own: and they would often ingenuously confess that he was certainly in the right way, and that they could not but wish they could live as he lived.

These men on their return to England spoke of him in the highest terms of applause to their respective families and connections. The Italian merchants also and the English factors resident in different parts of Italy, with whom he had transactions on money concerns, all wrote of him to their correspondents in England, with the warmest commendations, considering him as one who had some great object in view, and would some time appear to the world possessed of very extraordinary talents. Thus his reputation became general: on the exchange, in the city, at Court, and all over the country he was universally known and universally admired.

Having now finished his intended studies, having traversed all Italy, and become intimately acquainted with every place of consequence, being perfect master of the Italian language, both for writing and discourse, having an accurate knowledge of all their laws, customs, manners, doctrines, and practices, civil, and ecclesiastic, and having made the best use of everything he had heard, read, or seen, and being determined as to his future plan of conduct, he resolved at last to pay a visit to Imperial Rome. He knew indeed before he went thither, as much of that celebrated city, both ancient and modern, as could be learned from history, and from conversation with many persons of great judgment and observation, who had lately been there: but he was desirous to confirm what he had learned by information from others, by his own observation.

He stayed at Rome about ten days, and in that time he so improved his opportunities as that he satisfied himself in seeing all that he desired. But the particulars need not be here recited, as they may be found in many other books upon this subject.

From Rome he returned to Venice, not acquainting any one where he had been. At his return he was welcomed home by the Englishmen, and all his other acquaintance; as was the custom with them at other times, after his other excursions. In one of these, he went to see the Chapel of Loretto. From thence he went to Malta, where one of the Knights conceiving a particular friendship for him, at their parting desired his acceptance of one of the rich crosses worn by the brethren of that Order, entreating him to keep it for his sake; and thus exchanging mutual good wishes and benedictions, Mr. Ferrar returned again to Venice.

And now intending at length to leave Italy, he went from Venice to Marseilles, purposing after he had passed sufficient time in that city, for visiting what was remarkable there and in the parts adjacent, to take ship there and sail from thence to Spain.

But at Marseilles he fell dangerously ill, being suddenly seized with a violent fever, which daily grew worse and worse. And what added to his misfortune, he knew no one in the place, nor had he any of his former acquaintance with him. In this distress he sent for the most celebrated physician in the city, and trusted himself entirely to his care. He was very regular in his attendance, and was very careful of him. His host also and hostess where he lodged showed great tenderness and attention to him.

The first day he was taken ill he wrote to his much-loved friend whom he had left at Venice, the unfortunate Mr. Garton, to whom he had promised to give information of his arrival at Marseilles. In this letter he acquainted him that he was beginning to grow ill, and feared his illness would prove both long and dangerous. Nor was he mistaken, for his illness continued thirty-four days, and his physician was for a long time in absolute despair of his life. This made his attendants desirous to know who he was, which Mr. Ferrar industriously concealed. But one day, as they were looking amongst his things for something he had called for, carefully wrapped up in a little box was discovered the rich cross which was presented to him by his friend the Knight of Malta, at his departure from that Island. At sight of this, the host and hostess, and the physician presently concluded that he was a knight of that Order, who was travelling unknown, and they earnestly entreated him no longer to conceal himself. Mr. Ferrar in vain endeavoured to convince them of the mistake, assuring them that he was only a private gentleman, travelling for amusement and instruction; for the more he affirmed this, the more they were confirmed in their own opinion. His disorder still continuing excessive, the physician had given him up for lost. But at the very moment when all hope was gone, a favourable crisis took place; and though he was extremely weak, and reduced to the lowest degree, yet he soon appeared to be in a fair way of recovery.

And now word was brought to him that there was a gentleman below, just arrived from Venice, who demanded to see him. They who know what true friendship is, need not to be informed that this person could be no other than his dear and unfortunate friend Mr. Garton. When he came into Mr. Ferrar's room, and beheld his friend lying on the bed of sickness, so pale, weak, and reduced, he burst into tears. His friend was equally affected, seeing him so unexpectedly. They mutually embraced, and a long, and affectionately expressive silence ensued: for their hearts were so full, that neither could for some time speak to the other. At length Mr. Ferrar told him how welcome he was to him, who but yesterday expected never to see him more. Mr. Garton replied, that on the receipt of his letter he became so deeply afflicted, that he could not rest, day or night, till he should see him, in order that if he should find him still sick, he might abide with him and take care of him: that if he should die, he might perform the due honours of burial: and that if he should recover, he might rejoice with him on that happy occasion, and in every respect show him that unfeigned friendship which was justly due to his uncommon virtue.

As a sincere and affectionate friend is perhaps the most effectual medicine that can be administered to the sick, so by the endearing attentions of the benevolent Mr. Garton, Mr. Ferrar every day advanced apace in his recovery. And when he was thought to be out of danger, Mr. Garton said he must at last bid him farewell, and return to Venice. "Yes," said Mr. Ferrar, "you shall now return to Venice, but I will return with you. For as you have been so very kind as to come so far to take care of me when I was ill, and have likewise stayed so long with me, it is but justice, and the least return I can make, to see you safe back;" nor would he take any refusal; and so they returned together to Venice. From this place Mr. Ferrar immediately gave his parents an account of his cruel sickness and his recovery at Marseilles, in a very affectionate letter bearing date April, 1616.

Having stayed at Venice till he was perfectly recovered, and his strength thoroughly recruited, he took his last leave of all his friends and acquaintance there; but particularly of his dear friend Mr. Garton, who at their parting presented him with an excellent and costly rapier, saying that perhaps it might be of use to him in his future travels, and wished him to keep it as a testimony of his friendship. And now these dear friends with the warmest affection bade each other adieu. For in the gulf of Venice a small English vessel was ready to sail for Spain, and Mr. Ferrar resolved to take his passage in her, that so he might travel through Spain, and see that kingdom, after which he purposed in like manner to see France, and so return home.

The ship, in which Mr. Ferrar left Venice, carried only ten guns, but was over-loaded, though there were no passengers but himself. They had not been long at sea, before a large ship, a Turkish pirate, gave them chace, and gained speedily upon them. And there being some difference of opinion between the officers, and mariners, whether they ought to yield, or fight it out; they referred their doubts to Mr. Ferrar, who had stood silent among them attending to their debate. They said, "This young man has a life to lose, as well as we; let us hear what he thinks of the matter." For from his first coming on board, upon discourse with him, they had taken a great liking to him, perceiving that he had great skill in maritime affairs.

Mr. Ferrar being thus applied to in form for his opinion, resolutely told them that they ought to fight it out, and put their trust in GOD. That it was better to die valiantly, than be carried into slavery. That GOD could easily deliver them, and he hoped would not suffer them to fall into the hands of their enemy. He then put them in mind of the many sea engagements achieved by their countrymen, in which the victory had been gained against superior numbers. Thus encouraged, his words were so prevalent, that with all speed they made ready to defend themselves, committing their cause to the protection of God. And to show that they were not deficient in English spirit, they, having the advantage of the wind, and a fit opportunity, determined to give their enemy a broadside: when, lo! just as the master was giving the word to the gunner to fire, the Turkish ship, to their great astonishment, fell off, and steered away from them with all the sail she could make. They soon perceived that this unexpected movement was from the discovery of another ship, which, they supposed, was thought to be a better booty. The Turk being gone they proceeded on their voyage, and without any further difficulty arrived at their destined port in Spain.

Soon after his arrival, Mr. Ferrar determined to see Madrid, and the King's Court, and whatever else was worth notice in that part of the country. But having spent some time at Madrid, he had also spent almost all the money which he brought with him from Venice. He therefore made inquiry whether there were any bills of exchange, or letters for him, directed to some of the English merchants in that city, but could not hear of any; for he had reached Madrid long before his father thought he could be there. In making this inquiry, he carried the matter so, as if it was for a gentleman of the name of Ferrar, who he expected would be there

about that time: for he was resolved, if possible,
not to discover himself. But it happened that a
Mr. Wyche, the son of a merchant, a particular friend
of Mr. Ferrar's father, was at that time at Madrid.
And he being informed that this young stranger
made frequent inquiry after one of the name of
Ferrar, kept an observant eye upon him. And
perceiving something very extraordinary in his
genteel deportment, in the wisdom and the wit of his
conversation, and his great knowledge in languages,
he concluded him to be some person of high fashion,
who was desirous to travel unknown; and thereupon, both himself, and all the English established
there, made him an offer of all the civilities in their
power.

But as he was now at a stand how to proceed,
and what course to take in order to pass through
Spain, and then through France home, and being
uneasy that no bills of exchange were come for such
a one as he inquired after, he suddenly determined
to travel no farther at present; but immediately to
make the best of his way to England, and in order
to this, to travel on foot as well as he could to
S. Sebastian's, and there take ship for his native
country.

In preparation for this expedition, as he still resolved, if possible, to keep himself unknown, he

privately sold his cloak, and some jewels which he had by him, to supply his present occasions, and provide for his future wants in his journey. At quitting Madrid he took leave of Mr. Wyche, and the other English merchants, with acknowledgments of their many civilities to him. At which time Mr. Wyche made him an offer of what money he might want, which Mr. Ferrar politely declined.

And now he set forward on foot, with the rich rapier in his hand presented to him by his dear friend Mr. Garton, without a cloak, in his doublet and cassock. And with many a weary step, and very few accommodations, he pursued his journey, till he found his feet after a few days' travelling on the hot sands of that country to become quite wearied, and the skin to come off, so that it was excessively painful to him to proceed. One night his hostess where he lodged, seeing he was a young foot traveller, and that he suffered greatly from the torment of his feet, prescribed to him to bathe and steep his feet for a considerable time in a bowl of sack which she brought for that purpose. This gave him immediate ease, and enabled him to proceed comfortably on his journey the next morning, and by future applications prevented all future inconveniences of that sort.

His reason for travelling always with his rapier in his hand, was not only to be instantly upon his defence in case of any sudden attack, but that he might also pass the more readily in all places as a young soldier, going towards Flanders to serve the King of Spain, under Spinola. And upon the way at all fit times, and places, as he travelled, he seemed to be very inquisitive about Spinola, and what he was doing in Flanders; so that all with whom he had any discourse of this sort, took him for an Italian. But at one place where he passed the night, the governor being informed of a stranger, who lodged in the town, examined him strictly in many particulars. And Mr. Ferrar made him such wary answers, that he was at a loss what farther to say to him. At last casting his eyes upon the rapier, he told him that costly rapier was unbefitting him, for he knew not how he came by it, and therefore he would have it from him. Mr. Ferrar told him he must pardon him in not parting with his weapon, which a soldier ought to preserve as his life; adding that it was given him by a dear and worthy friend, who enjoined him to keep it, and that he was determined so to do. But this did not satisfy the governor, who told him that stout as he was he should deliver the rapier to him before he departed, or he would make him repent his refusal.

Mr. Ferrar replied, that he hoped there was more justice to be found everywhere in Spain, than to take by force an innocent traveller's weapon from him. That he had not in anything offended Cæsar, or his laws, or the customs of his country since he was in it, and that he would be cautious not to do so during the remainder of his stay. That he came very lately from the King's Court, and that he had friends there who would not suffer him to receive any wrong. From this wise and resolute answer, his determined behaviour, and a style of language so far above his outward appearance, the standers by concluded him to be some other man than his habit declared, and advised the governor to meddle no more with him about the rapier. Who then addressing himself to Mr. Ferrar, said, "Well, I perceive you are a young Italian gentleman, and inquire after our affairs in Flanders, and after the Marquis Spinola your countryman, to whom I understand you are going. I like well your weapon, which in truth is most handsome and soldier-like;" and so he dismissed him to proceed on his journey.

While Mr. Ferrar travelled thus alone over a great part of Spain, he walked once half a day without seeing anybody, and was therefore obliged to guess at his way by the best observation he could make, to proceed straight forward from the place where he had lodged the night before. And it being now near evening, he perceived that the road he was in led him to a very high hill, which at length he with no small pains and difficulty ascended: and being arrived at the top, he there found a round plat of level ground, of considerable magnitude, encompassed entirely with rocks of a prodigious height, and extremely steep on every side, neither could he discern any pathway, except that by which he had ascended, to lead him out from this rocky enclosure, and thereby encourage him to go forward.

At the sight of this he was much troubled, thinking he had wholly mistaken the hill which he had been directed to ascend, and that he must at last take up his unhoused lodging there that night. Being thus perplexed, and not knowing what to do, he devoutly knelt down, and prayed to GOD to protect and direct him. Then examining with careful anxiety all parts, to see if he could find any way to help him forward in his journey, for it was too late to think of returning, he espied a large black hog come hastily running out from a narrow crevice or cleft in the rock, and immediately disappear again. But he with his eyes observed, and with his feet made all possible haste to follow and see what was become of the beast. For he conceived hopes that it might be some tame animal, now in the evening returning to its home, and consequently, that possibly there was some dwelling-house not far off. Presently he saw the same creature again, now running at the farther end of the level plain down the side of the hill. And, coming to the spot, he perceived a hollow, covered passage, cut into the solid rock, and at some distance within this hollow, a sort of window or air-hole, to give light and air to this subterranean passage. Resolving therefore to follow the animal which he plainly saw to enter this cavity, after some time, and very cautious treading, he found a turning which grew at every step more and more dark. Yet stopping a little while, listening, and still looking and venturing slowly more forward, he discerned, as he thought, a glimmering of more light at a distance. So he went on, and found it to be another window or air-hole, cut like the former through the solid rock to give farther light to the subterranean passage. Thus proceeding onwards, in the same manner, and under the same disagreeable circumstances, he at length plainly perceived that this passage was a way to some subterranean habitation, cut by human labour into the heart of the rock. Thereupon, listening, and proceeding with caution, he fancied that he heard the voices of people talking at no great distance. Resolving therefore to go forward again, he found at length that there was indeed a sort of house in the very substance of the rock, and that it was a harbour, or place of entertainment for passengers who travelled that way.

Coming into the room he saluted the host, and the people who were there; and sitting down he called for bread and wine, and then began to discourse with them how hard it was to find the way to them: which, they said, to a stranger must be indeed extremely difficult, but was not so to those who were acquainted with the turns and windings of that subterranean labyrinth. He then called for more wine to wash and bathe his feet. Which done, after some communication of ordinary matters, such as travellers use with their hosts, he made strict observation of the disposition and manners of the people in the house, and found great reason not very well to like them: but now there was no remedy.

As for the people, they thought him to be a young Italian soldier, going to the Marquis Spinola. For that way his conversation much tended, and showed that he was well acquainted with all the military transactions in Flanders with the Hollanders. At length he told them that he was very weary and very sleepy, and, if they pleased, would lie down upon a bench, and take some rest. For that, he pretended, was his custom when he travelled in order to inure himself to hardships.

Thereupon they showed him into another room within the cavern; and Mr. Ferrar, not laying his rapier away, but keeping it close to him, lay down to sleep. But he was scarce laid down, when two lusty, ruffian looking fellows, and a young woman came into the room. Mr. Ferrar heard and saw them, but lay still, as if he was fast asleep. The men then demanded of the people of the house, "Who is this here, who lies sleeping upon the bench?" They answered, "We know not, he is lately come in very weary, and says he is a young Italian soldier, who is going into Flanders, to serve under Spinola." And then they entered into some conversation in a very low voice, which Mr. Ferrar could not hear.

After this they sat down at a table at the farther end of the room, and in a bold manner began to call for various things, and in drinking their wine they discoursed of different matters, and at length grew very merry. But at last one of the fellows went out, and after a short time came in again, and then after some slight and foolish words began to quarrel with the woman. She gave him as cross words in return, and their other companion taking her part, from words they came to blows, and began to lay hands on the woman. Whereupon she crying out, the host came running in, but instead of being appeased by him, they grew more and more fierce. All this Mr. Ferrar heard and saw, but appeared as if he was in a sound sleep, and kept his hand fast upon his rapier. They called to him for help, but he regarded not their brawling, still making as if he was dead asleep. Therefore as he continued to lie still, and seemed to take no notice of them, their contention ceased, and they all went out of the room in very friendly terms together.

Mr. Ferrar saw all this was done to provoke him to rise, and take one part or other, that so they might have quarrelled with him, and carried into execution some bad design against him. But he heard no more of them; and not being able to sleep, he rose at daybreak, and made haste away, giving GOD thanks for his escape out of their hands.

After his escape from this subterranean abode, having travelled five hundred miles in Spain, in the heat of summer, alone, and on foot, making his observations on the country, its curiosities, and productions, and on the disposition, and manners of the people, he at length arrived safely at S. Sebastian's. Here he found a ship ready to sail for England, but waiting for a fair wind. In this interval he received great civilities from the captain of the vessel, and from all the English settled at that place. At length the wind came fair, and after a few days' happy passage he landed at Dover, where he returned his sincere thanks to GOD for bringing him in health and safety to his native country.

CHAPTER III.

WE are now no longer to consider Mr. Ferrar as a young man travelling for amusement and instruction, displaying everywhere uncommon abilities, illustrious virtue, and indefatigable industry, exciting the highest admiration, and receiving in every country universal applause; but we shall now see him the man of business, applying with unwearied attention the great talents with which GOD had blessed him, to important negotiations both of a private and a public nature.

His return was at a very critical time. For one branch of his family was in great distress, and stood in need of his care and wisdom. His brother John Ferrar was likewise entered into a great public employment, by which he became engaged in many affairs which required his assistance. For Sir Edwyn Sandys being chosen Governor of the Virginia Company, Mr. John Ferrar was made King's Counsel for that plantation. He therefore left the management of his concerns in merchandise to his friends and partners. And the Virginia courts after this were kept at the house of Mr. Ferrar the father ; who from his singular affection for that honourable company, himself being one of the first adventurers of that plantation and the Somers Islands, allowed them the use of his great hall, and other best rooms of his house to hold their weekly and daily meetings. Many other things both of public and private concernment, now on foot, seemed equally to call for the presence and assistance of Mr. N. Ferrar. For (not to speak of public matters) to all human appearance, without his advice, diligence, and great wisdom in managing the private affairs of his family at this critical juncture, there had been great danger not only of much loss in many particulars, but even of the overthrow and ruin of his elder brother.

Immediately after his arrival at Dover Mr. Ferrar rode post to London ; and finding the door of his father's house open, he entered with his rich rapier at his side, arrayed only in his cassock and doublet, and just in the manner as he had travelled from Madrid to S. Sebastian's.

The meeting between the worthy parents and their beloved son, whom they had not seen for five years, and whom they had expected never to have seen again, was mutually affectionate and endearing to the highest degree, and may more easily be imagined than described. This his unexpected and much wished for return was in the year 1618; he himself being then twenty-six, his father seventy-two, and his mother sixty-two years of age.

He soon showed himself upon the exchange, and in person returned his thanks to those merchants by whose factors he had received his remittances, and many local civilities. He was now much noticed both for the beauty of his person, and for his many eminent qualities: and all his friends soon found that the accounts they had received of his worth and wisdom from abroad had not been exaggerated, but that his virtues, and his accomplishments surpassed all report, and all expectation.

In his travels through Holland, Germany, Italy and Spain, Mr. Ferrar purchased many rare articles of curiosity, many scarce and valuable books, and learned treatises in the languages of those different countries—in collecting which he certainly had a principal eye to those which treated the subjects of a spiritual life, devotion, and religious retirement. He bought also a very great number of prints engraved by the best masters of that time; all relative to historical passages of the Old and New Testaments. Indeed he let nothing of this sort that was valuable escape him. And this great treasure of rarities, books, and prints, upon his return home, he had the satisfaction to find were safely arrived there before him.

It now comes in the order of time to speak of the great hand which Mr. N. Ferrar had, immediately after his return, in the management of the affairs of the Virginia Company; in which, by his prudent conduct, he got through many and great difficulties with high credit and reputation.

Soon after Mr. Ferrar's return, Sir Edwyn Sandys who had heard a high character of him from many who had known him in Italy, sought his acquaintance; and being exceedingly taken with his great abilities, took the first opportunity to make him known to the Earl of Southampton, and the other principal members of the Virginia Company. In a very little time he was made one of a particular committee in some business of great importance; whereby the company having sufficient proof of his extraordinary abilities, at the next general court it was proposed and agreed that he should be King's

Counsel for the Virginia plantation in the place of his brother John, who was then made the Deputy Governor. And when his name, according to custom, was entered in the Lord Chamberlain's book, Sir Edwyn Sandys took care to acquaint that Lord with his uncommon worth: which indeed daily more and more appeared in everything he undertook: and as he wanted no ability, so he spared no diligence in ordering all their affairs of consequence. And thus he became deeply engaged in cares of a public nature. Yet his own inclinations at his return led him rather to think of settling himself at Cambridge, to which he was the more induced, as he still held the Physic Fellowship in Clare Hall. But this he now saw could not be done. Besides, his parents, now grown old, requested their beloved son to remain with them. Therefore all he could obtain in this respect from them, and from his business, was the liberty now and then to pass a few days with his old acquaintance and friends still remaining in Cambridge.

At this time, 1619, Mr. Henry Briggs, the celebrated Mathematician, and Reader of Geometry at Gresham College, and one of the Virginia Company, being about to leave London, and settle at Oxford as Savilian Professor there, recommended it to the City of London, who had the gift of that professorship, that they should by all means offer the place to Mr. Ferrar upon his own terms, saying, That he was the ablest proficient he knew in that science. The offer was made accordingly, which Mr. Ferrar modestly declined, saying his friend Mr. Briggs was much mistaken in him, and that his affection and goodness to him had misled his judgment. He therefore prayed them to appoint some more worthy person; but that for himself, though he declined the intended honour, he would always be ready to serve the City of London, and the magnificent foundation of Sir Thomas Gresham, to the utmost of his power.

While Sir Edwyn Sandys continued Governor, the reputation of the Virginia Company rose very high under his prudent management. But having now served his year, and being by the general voice intended to have been elected again, by some secret power at Court all the measures were broken that had been before taken for that purpose.

Sir Edwyn Sandys having been thus set aside, the Earl of Southampton was chosen governor, with Mr. John Ferrar as deputy. This nobleman had a particular friendship with Sir Edwyn Sandys, and took this office conditionally that his friend should continue his advice and assistance in the business of the company. So that there were now three very able men engaged, Lord Southampton, Sir Edwyn Sandys, and Mr. Nicolas Ferrar. Lord Southampton celebrated for wisdom, eloquence, and sweet deportment; Sir Edwyn Sandys for great knowledge and integrity; and Nicolas Ferrar for wonderful abilities, unwearied diligence, and the strictest virtue.

The latter was now fully employed in drawing up instructions concerning all the various business respecting the plantation, in writing all letters of advice to the colony in Virginia, and in being constantly one in every committee. These instructions and letters being always read in the open courts, gained him universal approbation. The civilians, the common lawyers, the divines, (of which last Dean Williams, afterwards Bishop of Lincoln, was one,) who attended these courts, when acquainted with Mr. Ferrar's performances, all spoke of him in highest terms of commendation. The merchants and tradesmen, when he had occasion to speak of their matters, even the sea officers and mariners, when he gave directions about the victualling and ordering the ships or other naval affairs, all were in the highest admiration of his abilities and accurate knowledge of everything relating to their respective professions. And now under the management and direction of Lord Southampton, Sir Edwyn

Sandys, and Mr. Nicolas Ferrar, the affairs of the Virginia plantation were soon in the most flourishing situation.

At this time there was in London a Mr. Copeland, a Minister in the Somers Islands, who contracted a great intimacy with Mr. Ferrar. He was a worthy man, and very zealous for the conversion of the infidel natives of America. He had many conferences with Mr. Ferrar upon this subject, and the best way and means to effect it ; and he seriously informed Sir E. Sandys and others of the company, that he verily believed Mr. Ferrar was determined some time to leave the old world, and settle in Virginia, and there employ the extraordinary talents with which GOD had blessed him, and spend his life in the conversion of the natives, or other infidels in that country :. adding, " If he should do so, I will never forsake him, but wait upon him in that glorious work." This appears a strong presumptive proof, that notwithstanding Mr. Ferrar's great abilities in different occupations, and his wonderful proficiency in various acquisitions of science, and other accomplishments, yet that the peculiar bent and determination of his mind was uniformly given to the promotion of the Christian religion.

At this time (April, 1620) died Mr. Ferrar the

father, who made his son Nicolas his sole executor. This was a great addition to the business already lying upon him : but he had abilities equal to anything, and to everything, together with firmness of mind and integrity equal to his ability. Mr. Ferrar, Senior, by his will gave £300 towards erecting a school or college in Virginia for the better education of such infidel children as should be there converted to the Christian religion. He was buried in the church of S. Bennet Sherhog, April 12, and his old friend Dr. Francis White, whom he brought from the obscurity of the country into a more public life, preached his funeral sermon to a crowded audience ; in which he described him as a second Nathaniel, an Israelite indeed in whom was no guile.

The Virginia plantation, now under the government of the Earl of Southampton, became every day of higher reputation, and the affairs of the company in consequence every day of more weighty importance. So that Mr. Ferrar, both as counsel to the company, and assistant also to his brother as deputy governor, was pressed by a double weight of care. Still the company would not permit the deputy to resign till he had executed his office three years, which he did, viz. 1619, under Sir Edwyn Sandys, and 1620, 1621, under the Earl of Southampton.

But now the increasing fame of this company, and the wise management of it was carried into Spain, and caused no small alarm. The politicians there saw, or pretended to see, danger in the course of not many years. Virginia was too near them, both by sea and land; and they did not know but the people of that plantation, when once a little settled, might perhaps be looking over the hills, and at length spy out their rich mines. Gondomar therefore, the Spanish Ambassador, had it in commission to have a special eye upon the company, and the managers of their affairs. And he was indeed a vigilant observer of his instructions. He not only gained an absolute influence over the King, but many great men about him, whom he had bought with Spanish money: these were very powerful, and well known at Court by the name of the Spanish party.

Gondomar and the King had now agreed upon the destruction of the Virginia Company. Notice of their designs was given to Lord Southampton and Sir Edwyn Sandys, by the Marquis of Hamilton and the Earl of Pembroke; who privately warned them to look well to themselves, and their proceedings, for that many stratagems were now in train, and would be pushed to the utmost to procure the destruction of the plantation, and to ruin all persons who should be employed in supporting the affairs of the company. This opportune advice produced a double care and watchfulness in the managers, if possible to prevent the intended mischief.

In the Easter term, 1622, Mr. John Ferrar having been continued deputy governor three years, Nicolas Ferrar was elected to succeed him. Indeed Lord Southampton had plainly told the deputation from the company, who waited on him to desire he would consent to be re-elected, that if they did not choose Mr. Nicolas Ferrar to be the deputy governor, he could not any longer take the office of governor upon him. He considered that Mr. Ferrar was the only person who was able to go through with the business: and to encounter all those great and potent oppositions, which he knew either were, or very soon would be raised against the company and the plantation; and that without Mr. Ferrar's assistance all would fall to ruin. "You all," he continued, "see and know his abilities and his integrity as well as I. On condition of his being deputy, I will be your governor: but he must be the person who must act both mine and his own part also. Without him I dare not accept the office; with him, I will do all I can to serve you."

These things being thus settled, the meetings at

Mrs. Ferrar's house began again to be crowded, as usual; and Gondomar exerted double diligence, procuring by Spanish gold, spies, who informed him of everything that was done at these meetings; and what added greatly to his influence, the Spanish party at Court carried everything with a high hand.

But by Mr. Ferrar's care and industry things seemed, notwithstanding, to be getting again in a fair way towards a lasting settlement.

After a short time, however, a commission was granted by the King to some known enemies to the company to disturb and tease them by vexatious examinations. And one Captain Butler, whom the company had removed from his office for scandalous mismanagement and injustice, was suborned, and made an instrument to spread disadvantageous reports of the country itself, as unfit to be planted, being extremely unhealthy and entirely unproductive.

Before these commissioners Mr. Ferrar often appeared in the defence of the company, and exerted himself with such firmness and force of argument, not only face to face to the accusers, but by such unanswerable deductions in writing, that the commissioners were not able to proceed: all their allegations being demonstrated by him to be false and frivolous. The matter therefore was brought from them before the Council table. And then Mr. Ferrar and the company were forced to attend there twice or thrice a week for half a year together, in order to weary them out by a vexatious persecution. But notwithstanding all these infamous machinations, nothing could be taken hold of to wrest the patent from the company. They were often indeed required to lay it down; but this they refused to do.

At this time, though there were many able men of the company ready to defend their just cause, yet the Lords of the Council insisted that the deputy, being, as they said, the representative of the company, should be the only person to answer their objections. And this they did on seeing him so young a man, thinking from that circumstance to gain some advantage over him. But he answered them all with that singular wisdom and modesty, that accurate knowledge of affairs, that discretion, firmness, and eloquence, that the mercenaries of Gondomar were confounded; and then by a new and unexpected artifice, and in pretended admiration of his great abilities, said it was pity but that he should be taken off from his present business, and employed in public affairs of more weighty importance.

Accordingly overtures were made, and a negotiation entered upon with Lord Southampton and Sir Edwyn Sandys, to prevail with them to persuade

Mr. Ferrar to accept the place of Clerk of the Council, or (Leiger) Envoy to the Duke of Savoy, which of the two employments he himself liked best. He modestly declined the offer, saying his abilities were not sufficient for a post of such weighty importance. His friends continued to press him and he to refuse. At length he told them that he could not accept of such preferment, that his thoughts lay quite another way. But seeing their importunity continue, he in confidence to his two great friends, and on their promise of secrecy, declared to them his solemn determination, when he should have discharged the duties of his present situation, to enter upon a state of religious retirement.

Still however the same unjust persecution of the company was carried on; and Mr. Ferrar still remained unanswerable in his defence. At length one day the Lord Treasurer Cranfield in great heat of passion told him, that he could prevail with the company if he would, and they might then obtain all that they desired.

Nicolas Ferrar then being called to the upper end of the Council table, addressed himself with all humility to the Lords, and to Lord Cranfield in particular, beseeching them in the most earnest manner not to entertain so vain an imagination.

That there were many members of the company much better qualified than he was to speak upon their affairs. Nevertheless, that he humbly entreated their Lordships to consider seriously, whether, if such a number of the Virginia Company as made a court, or whether, if all those members who lived in and near London, should meet and assemble together, whether even all these could either in law or equity give up the patent, without the previous consent of all the rest of the members, to the number of some thousands now dispersed all over England. And these too not persons of inferior rank, but persons of the first condition, of the nobility and gentry, of the bishops and clergy, of the chief citizens, and of the principal companies and corporations throughout the whole kingdom. Besides these, all the planters also in Virginia, who were all included in the grant, and who all upon the encouragement, and promised protection of the King, under the Great Seal of England, and the pledge of his royal word and honour, adventured their estates, and many of them even their lives in this the greatest and most honourable undertaking in which England had ever been engaged. He represented also the great good which in numberless sources of wealth and strength, would by means of this corporation, and through the encouragement of their care, by the blessing of GOD, shortly accrue to this nation. And he again and again most earnestly besought their Lordships to take all these things into their most serious consideration; and no longer to urge them, not the twentieth part of the persons interested, to do an action which was in itself both unjust and unreasonable, and indeed impossible for them to do. For how could they pretend to give away and yield up the rights and interests of other men, without the consent of the parties interested first obtained. And in the most solemn manner he adjured their Lordships not to make them the instruments of doing so vile a thing, to which if they consented, they should render themselves worthy of the severest punishment. "Besides," he said, "it is worthy your Lordships' farther consideration, how far such a precedent may possibly operate, and how dangerous such an example may be, if only a twentieth part of any company should presume, or should be permitted to deliver up the liberties and privileges, the rights, and the property of the other nineteen parts, and that without so much as once calling them together to give their consent." This, he continued, was what the company now assembled, must refuse as a thing unjust, and not feasible for them to do.

The Lord Treasurer upon his discoursing thus, being inflamed with violent passion, often interrupted him, and so did some others. But the Marquis of Hamilton, the Earl of Pembroke, and some other Lords of the Council said, "Nay, my good Lords, forbear. Let him make an end. We have called him hither to know what he can say on the company's behalf. Let us therefore not interrupt him: it is but reasonable to hear him out. Mr. Deputy, go on."

Mr. Ferrar, with the most respectful humility then said, "Most honourable Lords, I was just on the point of concluding. I will add only this, that as for my own private interest, and the interest of many here present, and of many others who are absent, my Lords, we all most humbly cast ourselves and our estates at his Majesty's royal feet: let him do with us and with them, if so he be determined, what seemeth best unto his good will and pleasure. For as to what is really our own, and in us to give, we submit it all to his Majesty's disposal; and in all other things we shall endeavour to serve and please him in all that with a conscience unhurt we may: desiring only this, that with respect to the rights and property of others, we may be permitted to execute the trust reposed in us, with fidelity and honour, and to discharge religiously those duties, which, as they are of the first importance, ought to have the first influence upon the mind of man."

Then the Marquis of Hamilton stood up, and with a loud voice said, "Mr. Deputy, in my opinion, my Lords, hath spoken well, excellently well both for himself, and for the company. And what, my Lords, can we now desire more of him?" The Earl of Pembroke seconded Lord Hamilton, and said, "Surely, my Lords, I hope the King (if he shall hear all) will be satisfied with what we have done, but particularly with what we have now heard. Let us fairly report it to him, and then let his Majesty do what he thinks most proper. We have sat a long time upon this business, and at length we may conjecture the result."

Gondomar with his profligate instruments, the King, and the Spanish party at Court, perceiving that Mr. Ferrar, (having demonstrated all their allegations to be false and groundless) had rendered all their violence ineffectual, now had recourse to a different mode of proceeding. They suborned, and procured persons to bring forward a crimination against him, who came and exhibited in form a complaint to the Council board. The substance of the accusation was this, That the deputy, during the times of his appearing before the Council, had drawn up and sent to the governor and plantation of Virginia certain dangerous instructions, and inflammatory letters of advice, directing them how they should conduct themselves in standing to their patent, and exhorting them that they should never give their consent to let it be delivered up. And therefore that if these letters and instructions were not countermanded by their Lordships, some very ill consequence might ensue, and the King might thereby receive much dishonour.

As soon as this pretended complaint was lodged in form, instantly, though it was then very late at night, some pursuivants, who were kept in readiness for that purpose, were despatched in all haste to Mrs. Ferrar's house to speak with the deputy, and to command him without any delay immediately to deliver up to them all those books of the Virginia Company wherein were registered the copies of all such letters and instructions as had been sent to the plantation from the council or company here.

Mr. Ferrar told them that the Secretary of the Virginia Company, and not he, had the keeping of those books. They then required him to give them a note to the secretary to deliver them. But he excused himself, saying, " Surely your commission will be a better authority for him to do so, than any note which I can send him. For my own part, if I had the company's evidences in my possession, entrusted to my custody, I certainly would *not* deliver them up, unless I had their leave, and express order so to do." When he said this they left him, and went to the secretary, and forced him to deliver up the books to them.

The next day the deputy, and many lords and gentlemen concerned in the company, were summoned to attend at the Council table. For the accusers of the company had given it out publicly that now very strange things indeed would be discovered in these books and instructions, and brought forth to public view. On this account there was a very numerous attendance, and all the Lords of the Council also were particularly summoned to attend.

When the Council was met, the deputy (as heretofore) was commanded to come to the upper end of the table. Then the accusers of the company desired of the Lords that one of the clerks of the Council might read such and such letters and instructions written in such and such months. Some of these being read, the Lords of the Council looked upon one another with evident marks of astonishment; observing that there was nothing of that dangerous consequence in those papers, which the accusers had informed them they would discover; but on the contrary much matter of high commendation. "Point out," said one lord, "where is the fault or error in these letters and instructions; for my own part I must say that I cannot see any."

The enemies of the company then prayed their lordships to hear them all read out; and then they said it would soon appear where the faults lay. "Yea, yea," said the Lord Treasurer with vehemence, "read on, read on: we shall anon find them." So they still persisted to read. And in a word, so much patience had the lords, or rather so much pleasure, that many of them said they thought their time had been well spent. All these letters and instructions being in the end thus read out, and nothing at all appearing which was any ways disadvantageous to the company, but on the contrary very much to their credit and honour; the Marquis of Hamilton stood up, and said, That there was one letter which he prayed might be read over again, on which he should desire to make a few observations. Which being accordingly done, "Well!" said he, " my lords, we have spent many hours here, in hearing all these letters and instructions, and I could not help requesting to hear this one letter over again; because I think that all your lordships must agree with me that it is absolutely a masterpiece. And indeed they are all in high degree excellent. Truly, my lords, we have this day lost no time at all. For I do assure you that if our attendance here were for many days, I for my part would willingly sit them out to hear so pious, so wise, and indeed politic instructions as these are. They are papers as admirably well penned as any I ever heard. And, I believe, if the truth were known, your lordships are all of the same opinion."

The Earl of Pembroke said, "There is not one thing in them all, which, as far as I can see, deserves in the least degree to be excepted against. On the contrary they all deserve the highest commendation: containing advices far more excellent than I could have expected to have met with in the letters of a trading company. For they abound with soundness of good matter, and profitable instruction with respect both to religion and policy; and they possess uncommon elegance of language." Many other lords concurred in these commendations, and at length one, addressing himself to Mr. Ferrar, said, "Mr. Deputy, I pray you tell us who penned these letters and instructions, we have some reason to think it was yourself."

Mr. Ferrar, whose modesty and humility were not inferior to his other rare accomplishments, replied, "My lord, these are the letters and instructions of the company, and the council of the company. For in all weighty affairs they order several committees to make each a rough draught of what they judge proper to be done in these matters: which rough draughts are afterward all put together, and presented first to the council, and then to the company to receive all proper alteration, as they shall please. And thus everything is drawn up and concluded upon the opinion and advice of many." After due commendation of his modesty as well as his ability, it was replied to him, "Mr. Deputy, That these papers before us are the production of one pen, is very plainly discernible: they are jewels that all come out of one rich cabinet, of which we have undoubted reason to believe that you are the true possessor."

The lords under the influence of Gondomar were now abashed and silent; only one of them said to the accusers of the company, "What strange and unaccountable measures are these that you have taken! to have us called together, and to make us sit and hear all these things, which are entirely opposite to your own informations, and which meet, as you find, with universal approbation." To this one man of a bold spirit replied, "We shall still in the end carry our point. These, my good lord, are not the letters and instructions which we meant. The company have others no doubt in private, which they secrete, and which if they could now be found, would quickly silence them. We have lately heard of things passing in their courts which would surprise you." Hereupon one of the council rose and said, "My lords, such malevolence and injustice is unequalled: such proceedings are not to be endured. But unprincipled malice has a face too brazen to be ashamed of anything." The lords then rose; and the adversaries of the company were much confounded, having now with all honest and impartial men entirely lost all credit.

The very night after this meeting, one of the clerks of the Council came to Lord Southampton and told him that his deputy had that day gained a most complete victory, and had extorted the highest commendations even from the lords of the adverse party: and it was supposed that proposals would be made to him to engage in the King's immediate service. "But for all that, my lord," said he, "depend upon it, such the times are, your patent is irretrievably gone."

Lord Southampton communicated this information to the lords and gentlemen interested in the company, saying, "You all well know that those things which our enemies thought would have been to their advantage and our damage, have hitherto all turned out to our credit and to our honour, nevertheless all will not help us. It is determined that our patent shall be taken away, and the company dissolved. The King, I find, has resolved to have the management of the plantation in his own hands, to direct, and govern as he sees best. A thing indeed worthy a King's care: but, alas! alas! this is all but a colourable show. For you will find in the end that this worthy company will be broken, and come to nothing. We must all arm ourselves with patience."

Mr. Ferrar had now gained the highest reputation with all ranks of men for the uncommon abilities which he displayed on every occasion: the esteem for his great virtues was unbounded, but especially with those who were interested in the affairs of the Virginia Company. At this time a citizen of the first class both for riches and reputation paid him a visit, and after the warmest expressions of the highest opinion of his extraordinary talents and integrity, thus continued: "Mr. Ferrar, I have an only daughter, who, if paternal affection doth not too much influence my judgment, is both wise and comely: indeed it is confessed by all that she is very beautiful: I know her to have been virtuously educated, to be well accomplished, and to be of an amiable disposition. If you will be pleased to accept of her as your wife, I will immediately give you with her ten thousand pounds."

Mr. Ferrar was much surprised, returned his sincere thanks, but said he was not worthy of so great a treasure. The citizen however persisted, said he was really in earnest to bring about the connection: that at present he only made his proposal with intent to give him an opportunity to consider of it. After a few days he came again, and asked Mr. Ferrar if he had advised with his friends concerning his proposal, saying, "They all know me well." Mr. Ferrar answered that he had not; "for you, I perceive, Sir, are greatly mistaken in me, first in having too high an opinion of my abilities, and next with respect to my estate, which you perhaps may conceive to be what it is not. I think myself infinitely obliged to you for your good will towards me, and for honouring me so far as to think, what I cannot think of myself, that I am any way worthy of so inestimable a treasure as your daughter." "Mr. Ferrar," he replied, "do not talk thus to me: for I know you perfectly well; and as for your estate, I give myself no manner of concern about it. What fortune you have I demand not to know. Let it be what it will; if you have nothing, I thank GOD that I have enough to make you and my daughter happy as to all worldly matters. And as to my own part, I shall think myself the happiest man upon earth to have you my son-in-law, and my daughter must be equally happy to have so accomplished, and so virtuous a man for her husband."

By means of an intimate friend of the father, an interview was brought about at this friend's house between the young lady and Mr. Ferrar, where in a select company they passed several hours together. The father then took a convenient opportunity to ask his daughter what she thought of Mr. Ferrar, to which she answered, "Nothing but good." "Can you then like him for a husband?" To which with equal ingenuousness and modesty she replied, " Sir, I shall with pleasure do in this, as well as in all other things, as you will please to have me: my duty and my inclination will go together." Matters being so far advanced, the father said to Mr. Ferrar, "Now, Sir, you have seen my daughter, I hope her person and deportment are such as to merit your approbation. As to your own estate, nothing is desired to be known. Be that as it may; I have enough; I like you, and my daughter submits herself to my choice. Now let me have your answer." Mr. Ferrar replied, "The young lady your daughter, Sir, is in every respect not only unexceptionable, but highly to be admired: she is beautiful and accomplished, and amiable to the greatest degree, and far superior to all that I can merit: indeed I do not, I cannot deserve this great happiness. I return you my sincerest thanks for your unequalled goodness to me; and in the confidence of friendship I will now acquaint you with the private and fixed determination of my mind. If GOD will give me grace to keep a resolution long since formed, I have determined to lead a single life; and after having discharged, to the best of my ability, my duty to the company, and to my family as to worldly concerns, I seriously purpose to devote myself to GOD, and to go into a religious retirement." Thus ended this affair, and the father ever after preserved the most affectionate friendship for Mr. Ferrar.

Mr. Ferrar's efforts, however, on behalf of the company were all in vain. For he, as deputy, and thirty more of the directors and principal persons of the Virginia Company were served with a writ of *Quo Warranto*, and commanded to show by what authority they pretended to exercise a power over the plantation, and send a governor thither: and by this process the company were now obliged to go to law to defend their rights. The case was given against them, the sentence being, "That the patent or charter of the company of English merchants trading to Virginia, and pretending to exercise a power and authority over his Majesty's good subjects there, should be thenceforth null and void."

The great reputation of Mr. Ferrar being now spread over all parts of the country by the members of the late dissolved Virginia Company, he was in 1624 elected a Member of Parliament. As this in a general consideration was highly proper on account of his extensive abilities, and known integrity; so was there a peculiar propriety in his election at this time; as there was an intention now to call to account before the House of Parliament, those persons who had abused the King's ear, and had been guilty of those violent enormities in the false accusation of the managers of the Virginia Company. For it was well known that Mr. Ferrar was not only more accurately acquainted with all the circumstances of that affair than any other person, but had also abilities and firmness sufficient to carry on the prosecution in a proper manner.

The Prince being now returned from Spain in great discontent, the Spanish party at Court began in some degree to lose their influence. The Parliament met. Mr. Ferrar was appointed one of several committees. Sir Edwyn Sandys, and many other members of the late Virginia Company were also in this Parliament. A charge was brought in against the Lord Treasurer, the Earl of Middlesex, for taking bribes, and divers other exorbitances committed in the execution of his office; and also for his conduct in the Virginia affair, and his violence in taking away the patent, and dissolving the company.

On this occasion the House appointed the Lord William Cavendish, Sir Edwyn Sandys, and Nicolas Ferrar to draw up the charge against him and those others, who had been his instruments in that scandalous proceeding. The charge was soon drawn up, as Mr. Ferrar had all the necessary materials ready in his hands. The accusation was opened by him in a speech which lasted two hours, and which gained him universal admiration. For now he was fully and publicly seen in this exertion of his great abilities. The Lord Treasurer was deprived of his office, and punished by a large fine and imprisonment.

The iniquity of the Virginia business being fully proved, and laid before the public, by Mr. Ferrar, and the other managers, the house resolved to take the whole affair into their serious consideration, and endeavour to restore the company. But before they could make any progress they received a message from the King, "That he both already had, and would also hereafter take the affair of the said late Virginia Company into his *own* most serious consideration and care: and that by the next Parliament they should all see he would make it one of his *masterpieces*, as it well deserved to be." And thus was all farther proceeding in that matter dishonourably stayed.

Mr. Ferrar having seen the dissolution of the Virginia Company, and no hope left of its revival, took his leave of the Virginia affairs by now paying the £300 left by his father for the purpose of erecting a College there, to the governor and company of the Somers Islands; binding them in articles to send for three Virginia children, and bring them up in those islands; and when of fit age to put them out to some proper business; or else educate them in learning and then send them back to the place of their birth, to convert their countrymen: and that when the first three were thus disposed of three others should from time to time be sent for in succession for the same benevolent purpose.

And thus ended Mr. Ferrar's public life, in which he displayed many proofs of great and extensive abilities, and of uncommon virtue, particularly of indefatigable diligence, industry, and activity, by which he gained universal admiration, and performed many important services, both to the Virginia Company, and all others with whom he was concerned.

CHAPTER IV.

THE King having seized the patent and dissolved the Virginia Company, and Mr. Ferrar having seen the attested copies of all the books and papers belonging to them delivered into safe custody in the Dorset family, he was now disengaged from public cares, and determined to carry into execution the plan he had long set his heart upon, to bid farewell to the busy world, and spend the remainder of his days in religious retirement, and a strict course of devotion.

Yet before he could complete his pious purpose it was necessary for him finally to settle some matters of great consequence, though of a private nature, which had been entrusted to his care. His established reputation for inflexible integrity had influenced several persons to prevail with him to undertake the executorship of their wills, and the settlement of their worldly affairs: and in some of these instances this trust concerned property of great value, and was involved in circumstances of great difficulty. Besides these occupations relative to the property of others, the situation of his brother required his immediate and close attention. Mr. John Ferrar had been for three years deputy governor of the Virginia Company, and in order to give himself up wholly to the discharge of that important trust, he had put into the hands of his partners in mercantile business seven thousand pounds, and assigned the management of those affairs over to them. He also advanced six thousand pounds more to them, for which he was engaged by a personal security. Whether it were by mismanagement or misfortune does not at present appear, but about this time the concerns of this partnership were fallen into the greatest confusion, and involved in the utmost embarrassment. Mr. N. Ferrar nevertheless by his great sagacity, and indefatigable industry, in a shorter time than could be believed, extricated his brother from all his difficulties, and settled his affairs in the most honourable manner at the loss of about three thousand pounds.

His next care was to provide a place fitted for the purpose and corresponding with his ideas of religious retirement. His mother had indeed a very large house in London, in which had been holden the meetings of the Virginia Company: she had also a considerable estate, and a large house in the town of Hertford. But neither of these places had his approbation, both being too much in view of the public.

At length he was informed that the Lordship of Little Gidding in the county of Huntingdon was to be sold. He immediately went thither to examine the place and premises, which he found with respect to privacy of situation exactly suited to his wishes. It was a parish that had been for some time depopulated. Nothing was left but one extremely large mansion house, going hastily to decay, and a small church within thirty or forty paces of the house, and at that time converted into a barn. Upon his return to London he purchased the whole lordship, and this purchase was made in the year 1624.

But now the plague having been some time in London, was in the year 1625 spread over most parts of the town, and was discovered to be at the very next door to Mrs. Ferrar's house. Mr. N. Ferrar was therefore very urgent that she and the family would immediately depart into the country: but while she lingered, being unwilling to leave him behind, he procured a coach and at length prevailed: and that very night, Whitsun-eve, she with her son John, and the rest of the family went to her house at Hertford, and the following week to her daughter Collet's, at Bourne Bridge in Cambridgeshire.

Mr. N. Ferrar would have attended his mother, but that he had not completely settled his brother's

NICOLAS FERRAR. 89

affairs. During this business, Mr. J. Ferrar, leaving his mother at Bourne, went to Gidding to make some necessary preparation there for the reception of the family, who were now become very unhappy at the stay of Mr. N. Ferrar in London, as they had been informed that the disorder was fatal every week to more than four thousand persons. As soon as he had finished the business which required his stay, he, with great joy and gratitude to GOD, repaired to Gidding: from whence he wrote to his mother entreating her not to come to him in less than a month, that it might appear whether he had brought away any infection with him. But her impatience to see him was so great, that three days after she rode thither, and their meeting was such as might, at that time, be expected between a pious parent and a dutiful son, to the highest degree mutually affectionate. In its circumstances indeed very different from the modern meetings of parent and son; for he, though twenty-seven years of age, who had been engaged in many public concerns of great importance, had been a distinguished Member of Parliament, and had conducted with effect the prosecution of the prime minister of the day, at first approaching his mother, knelt upon the ground to ask, and receive her blessing. Modern customs indicate a great change of manners with respect to the reverence then thought due to parents. He then besought her to go into the house, rude as it was, and repose herself. This she refused till she had given thanks to GOD in the church, which was very near at hand. But she was exceedingly grieved to find it filled with hay, and instruments of husbandry. Immediately all the workmen, many in number, employed in the repair of the house, were set to cleanse and repair the church: for she said, she would not suffer her eyes to sleep, nor her eyelids to slumber, till she had purified the temple of the LORD, and made it a habitation fit for the living GOD. In about a month's time, finding that all danger of infection was over, she sent for her beloved daughter Collet, and her husband, and all their numerous family to come and live with her at Gidding.

Mrs. Ferrar was now seventy-three years of age, yet was she possessed of so much vigour, and had so much of the appearance as well as the reality of health, that all who saw her concluded her to be not more than forty. Her family now consisted of near forty persons; and it being a season of deep humiliation on account of the mortality then become general all over the kingdom, it was determined to address themselves to GOD, as often as they conveniently could, according to the doctrine and discipline of the Church of England. To this end, Mr. N. Ferrar obtained permission of his old acquaintance Bishop Williams to have the service performed in the church, which was now put into decent repair; and he procured the minister of the adjoining parish to say the morning service every day at eight o'clock, the Litany at ten, and the evening service at four. On the Sunday morning the whole family went to Steeple Gidding, and in the afternoon, the minister of that parish, and his parishioners, came to the church newly repaired by Mrs. Ferrar.

At Easter, 1626, the plague being then ceased, Mr. N. Ferrar and his mother, and some other of the family went to London, to dispose of their great house there, to settle their remaining affairs, and to take a final leave of all their friends. When they had been some little time in London, he resolved, in order the better to carry on his religious plan by his own personal assistance, to become a Deacon. This resolution he communicated to none but his honoured tutor, Dr. Lindsel, who highly applauded it, and introduced him to Dr. Laud, the future Archbishop of Canterbury, then Bishop of S. David's, by whom he was ordained Deacon on the Trinity Sunday following.

On his return home he addressed himself to his mother, and showed her in a writing signed, a vow which he had made with great solemnity; That since GOD had so often heard his most humble petitions, and delivered him out of many dangers; and in many desperate calamities had extended His mercy to him; he would therefore now give himself up continually to serve GOD to the utmost of his power, in the office of a Deacon: into which office he had that very morning been regularly ordained. That he had long ago seen enough of the manners, and of the vanities of the world; and that he did hold them all in so low esteem, that he was resolved to spend the remainder of his life in mortifications, in devotion, and charity, and in a constant preparation for death.

There is reason to believe that even in his infancy, and before he set out upon his travels, and after his great escape upon the Alps, he did privately, and solemnly devote himself to GOD; and that after his unexpected recovery from his dangerous illness both at Padua, and Marseilles, he repeated these pious resolutions, adding also a vow of perpetual celibacy.

The news of Mr. Ferrar being ordained was soon spread abroad both in the city and at Court; as in both he was universally known and very highly esteemed. His constant friends the Marquis of Hamilton, Lord Pembroke, and Sir Edwyn Sandys took this opportunity of saying to him, That though he had formerly refused all temporal emoluments, yet now he had taken Orders, they must suppose that he had not any objection to spiritual preferment, and immediately made him an offer of some ecclesiastical benefices of great value. These he refused with steadiness and humility, saying that he did not think himself worthy. He added also that his fixed determination was to rise no higher in the Church, than the place and office which he now possessed, and which he had undertaken only with the view to be legally authorised to give spiritual assistance, according to his abilities, to his family or others, with whom he might be concerned. That as to temporal affairs, he had now parted with all his worldly estate, and divided it amongst his family. That he earnestly besought his honoured friends to accept his sincere thanks for their good opinion of him, for whose prosperity both in this world and a better he would never cease to pray. And now having finished all business in London, and taken a solemn and final leave of all their friends, he and his mother returned to Gidding.

It now comes in course to speak of the established economy both of the house and the church; and it is hoped that the reader will here excuse a circumstantial relation: because on these very circumstances, misapprehended, and misrepresented, were founded all the calumnies and persecution which the family afterwards suffered.

Many workmen having been employed near two years, both the house and church were in tolerable repair, yet with respect to the church Mrs. Ferrar was not well satisfied. She therefore new floored and wainscoted it throughout. She provided also two new suits of furniture for the reading desk, pulpit, and Communion Table: one for week days, the other for Sundays and other Festivals. The furniture for week days was of green cloth, with suitable cushions and carpets. That for festivals was of rich blue cloth, with cushions of the same, decorated with lace, and fringe of silver. The pulpit was fixed on the north, and the reading desk over against it, on the south side of the church, and both on the same level: it being thought improper that a higher place should be appointed for preaching, than that which was allotted for prayer. A new font was also provided, the leg, laver, and cover all of brass, handsomely and expensively wrought and carved; with a large brass lectern, or pillar and eagle of brass for the Bible. The font was placed by the pulpit, and the lectern by the reading desk.

The half-pace, or elevated floor on which the Communion Table stood at the end of the Chancel, with the stalls on each side, was covered with blue taffety, and cushions of the finest tapestry and blue silk. The space behind the Communion Table, under the east window, was elegantly wainscoted, and adorned with the Ten Commandments, the Lord's Prayer, and the Apostles' Creed, engraved on four beautiful tablets of brass, gilt.

The Communion Table itself was furnished with a silver paten, a silver chalice, and silver candlesticks, with large wax candles in them. Many other candles of the same sort were set up in every part of the church, and on all the pillars of the stalls. Mrs. Ferrar also taking great delight in Church music, built a gallery at the bottom of the church for the organ.[1] Thus was the church decently furnished, and ever after kept elegantly neat and clean.

All matters preparatory to order and discipline being arranged and settled, about the year 1631, Dr. Williams, the Bishop of Lincoln, came privately to Gidding, to pay a visit to his old friend Mr. N. Ferrar, with whom he had contracted a friendship at the Virginia board, and for whom he ever held the highest and most affectionate esteem.

By this visit he had an opportunity to view the

[1] These arrangements are not to be commended for correctness or taste, but only as acts of devotion and care of the House of God.

church, and the house, and to examine into their way of serving GOD, which had been much spoken against; to know also the soundness of the doctrine they maintained; to read the rules which Mr. N. Ferrar had drawn up for watching, fasting, and praying, for singing psalms and hymns, for their exercises in readings, and repetitions; for their distribution of alms, their care of the sick, and wounded; and all other regularities of their institution. All which the Bishop highly approved, and bade them in GOD's name to proceed.

In 1633 Mrs. Ferrar came to a resolution to restore the glebe lands and tithes to the Church, which some fourscore years before had been taken away, and in lieu thereof only £20 a year paid to the Minister. She had from the first been so resolved, but had been put off by unexpected delays. She found great difficulty in making out the glebe lands: but at length by the industry of Mr. N. Ferrar she overcame it. She then sent her sons John and Nicolas with a letter to the Bishop informing him of her determination, and desiring it might be confirmed by his authority. This authority from the Bishop was farther strengthened by a decree in chancery under Lord Coventry.

In the spring of 1634, the Bishop gave notice, that he would again pay a visit to the family and give them a sermon. And application was made to Dr. Towers, Dean of Peterborough, who sent his whole choir to Gidding on the occasion. Divine service was performed throughout in the cathedral manner with great solemnity. The Bishop preached a sermon adapted to the occasion, and in the afternoon gave Confirmation to all of the neighbourhood who desired it.

Everything relative to the church being now completely settled, Mr. Ferrar next turned his attention to the disposition of the mansion. The house being very large, and containing many apartments, he allotted one great room for their family devotions, which he called the Oratory, and adjoining to this, two other convenient rooms, one a night Oratory for the men, the other a night Oratory for the women : he also set out a separate chamber and closet for each of his nephews and nieces : three more he reserved for the schoolmasters; and his own lodgings were so contrived that he could conveniently see that everything was conducted with decency and order: without doors he laid out the gardens in a beautiful manner, and formed in them many fair walks.

Another circumstance that engaged his attention was, that the parish had for many years been turned into pasture grounds ; that as there was a very large

K

dovecote, and a great number of pigeons upon the premises, these pigeons must consequently feed upon his neighbours' corn; and this he thought injustice. He therefore converted this building into a schoolhouse, which being larger than was wanted for the young people of the family, permission was given to as many of the neighbouring towns as desired it, to send their children thither, where they were instructed without expense, in reading, writing, arithmetic, and the Principles of the Christian Religion.

For this and other purposes he provided three masters to be constantly resident in the house with him. The first was to teach English to strangers, and English and Latin to the children of the family: the second good writing in all its hands, and arithmetic in all its branches: the third, to instruct them in the theory and practice of music, in singing, and performing upon the organ, viol, and lute: on the last instrument his sister Collet was a distinguished performer.

For all these things the children had their stated times and hours. So that though they were always in action, and always learning something, yet the great variety of things they were taught prevented all weariness, and made everything be received with pleasure. And he was used to say that he who could attain to the well-timing things, had gained an important point, and found the surest way to accomplish great designs with ease.

On Thursdays and Saturdays, in the afternoons, the youths were permitted to recreate themselves with bows and arrows, with running, leaping, and vaulting, and what other manly exercises they themselves liked best. With respect to the younger part of the females, the general mode of education was similar to that of the boys, except where the difference of sex made a different employment or recreation proper. When the powers of reason and judgment became in some degree matured, they were all at proper times taken under the immediate instruction of Mr. Ferrar himself, who bestowed several hours every day in that important employment. According to the capacity of each he gave them passages of Scripture to get by heart, and particularly the whole book of Psalms. He selected proper portions, of which he gave a clear explanation, and a judicious comment. But above all things he was anxiously attentive to daily catechetical lectures, according to the doctrine of the Church of England. And in order to make his pious labours extensively beneficial, he invited the children of all the surrounding parishes, to get the book of Psalms by heart. To encourage them to this performance, each was presented with a Psalter: all were to repair to Gidding every Sunday morning, and each was to repeat his Psalm, till they could all repeat the whole book. These Psalm children, as they were called, more than a hundred in number, received every Sunday, according to the proficiency of each, a small pecuniary reward and a dinner, which was conducted with great regularity. For when they returned from church, long trestles were placed in the middle of the great hall, round which the children stood in great order. Mrs. Ferrar and her family then came in to see them served. The servants brought in baked puddings and meat: which was the only repast provided on Sundays for the whole family, that all might have an opportunity of attending divine service at church. She then set on the first dish herself, to give an example of humility. Grace was said, and then the bell rang for the family, who thereupon repaired to the great dining-room, and stood in order round the table. Whilst the dinner was serving, they sang a hymn to the organ: then grace was said by the minister of the parish, and they sat down. During dinner one of the younger people whose turn it was, read a chapter in the Bible, and when that was finished, another recited some chosen story out of the book of Martyrs, or Mr. Ferrar's short histories. When the dinner was finished throughout the family, at two o'clock the bell summoned them to church to evening service, whither they went in a regular form of procession, Mr. N. Ferrar sometimes leading his mother, sometimes going last in the train: and having all returned from church in the same form, thus ended the *public* employment of every Sunday.

Immediately after church the family all went into the Oratory, where select portions of the Psalms were repeated, and then all were at liberty till five o'clock: at which hour in summer, and six in winter, the bell called them to supper: where all the ceremonial was repeated exactly the same as at dinner. After supper they were again at liberty till eight, when the bell summoned them all into the Oratory, where they sang a hymn to the organ, and went to prayers; when the children asked blessing of their parents, and then all the family retired to their respective apartments; and thus ended the private observation of the LORD's Day.

On the first Sunday of every month they always had Holy Communion, which was administered by the clergyman of the adjoining parish; Mr. N. Ferrar assisting as deacon. All the servants who then received the Communion, when dinner was brought up, remained in the room, and on that day dined at the same table with Mrs. Ferrar, and the rest of the family.

When their early devotions in the Oratory were finished they proceeded to church in the following order,

First, the three schoolmasters, in black gowns, and Monmouth caps.

Then Mrs. Ferrar's grandsons, clad in the same manner, two and two.

Then her son Mr. J. Ferrar, and her son-in-law Mr. Collet, in the same dress.

Then Mr. N. Ferrar, in surplice, hood, and square cap, sometimes leading his mother.

Then Mrs. Collet, and all her daughters, two and two.

Then all the servants, two and two. The dress of all was uniform.

Then, on Sundays, all the Psalm children, two and two.

As they came into the church, every person made a low obeisance, and all took their appointed places. The masters, and gentlemen in the chancel: the youths knelt on the upper step of the half-pace: Mrs. Ferrar, her daughters and all her granddaughters in a fair island seat.[1] Mr. N. Ferrar at

[1] It is almost needless to remark that this specimen of internal arrangement is an incorrect one. The

coming in made a low obeisance; a few paces farther, a lower: and at the half-pace, a lower still: then went into the reading desk, and said matins according to the Book of Common Prayer. This service over, they returned in the same order, and with the same solemnity. This ceremonial was regularly observed every Sunday, and that on every common day was nearly the same. They rose at four; at five went to the Oratory to prayers; at six, said the psalms of the hour; for every hour had its appointed psalms, with some portion of the Gospel, till Mr. Ferrar had finished his Concordance, when a chapter of that work was substituted in place of the portion of the Gospel. Then they sang a short hymn, repeated some passages of Scripture, and at half-past six went to church to Matins. At seven said the psalms of the hour, sang the short hymn, and went to breakfast. Then the young people repaired to their respective places of instruction. At ten, to church to the Litany. At eleven to dinner. At which season were regular readings in rotation, from the Scripture, and from the book of Martyrs, and from short histories drawn up by Mr. Ferrar, and adapted to the pur-

Chancel is not intended for any that do not take an official part in the Service, i.e. only for the clergy and choir.

pose of moral instruction. Recreation was permitted till one; instruction was continued till three. Church at four, for evensong; supper at five, or sometimes six. Diversions till eight. Then prayers in the Oratory: and afterwards all retired to their respective apartments. To preserve regularity in point of time, Mr. Ferrar invented dials in painted glass in every room : he had also sundials, elegantly painted with proper mottos, on every side of the church : and he provided an excellent clock to a sonorous bell.

The short histories alluded to above were probably composed on the occasion, and to suit some present purpose. Those which are still remaining in my possession are put together without any regularity of series, or any dependence of one upon another, and are as in the catalogue annexed.

LIVES.

The Life of Monica.
Of Abraham.
Of Eliezer.
Of the Lady Paula.
Of Hyldegardis.
Of Paracelsus.
Of Dr. Whitaker.
Of Scaliger.

The Life of Mr. Perkins.
Of Dr. Metcalf.
Of Sir Francis Drake.
Of Mr. Cambden
Of Haman.
Of Wolsey.
Of Brandon Duke of Suffolk.

NICOLAS FERRAR. 105

The Life of Lord Burleigh.
Of Sir J. Markham.
Of S. Augustin.
Of Bishop Ridley.
Of Lady Jane Grey.
Of Queen Elizabeth.
Of Gustavus Adolphus.
Of the Black Prince.

The Life of Joan Queen of Naples.
Of the Witch of Endor.
Of Joan of Arc.
Of Cæsar Borgia.
Of John.
Of Andronicus Comnenus.
Of the Duke of Alva.

CHARACTERS.

The good Wife.
The good Husband.
The good Parent.
The good Child.
The good Master.
The good Servant.
The good Widow.
The constant Virgin.
The elder Brother.
The younger Brother.
The good Advocate.
The good Physician.
The controversial Divine.
The true Church antiquary.
The general Artist.
The faithful Minister.
The good Parishioner.
The good Patron.
The good Landlord.
The good Master of a College.

The good Schoolmaster.
The good Merchant.
The good Yeoman.
The Handicraftsman.
The good Soldier.
The good Sea-captain.
The good Herald.
The true Gentleman.
The Favourite.
The wise Statesman.
The good Judge.
The good Bishop.
The true Nobleman.
The Court Lady.
The Embassador.
The good General.
The heir apparent to the Crown.
The King.
The Harlot.
The Witch.

The Atheist.
The Hypocrite.
The Heretic.
The rigid Donatist.
The Liar.

The common Barrator.
The degenerous Gentleman.
The Pazzians' Conspiracy.
The Tyrant.

GENERAL RULES, OR ESSAYS.

CHAP.
1. Of Hospitality.
2. Of Jesting.
3. Of Self-praising.
4. Of Travelling.
5. Of Company.
6. Of Apparel.
7. Of Building.
8. Of Anger.
9. Of expecting Preferment.
10. Of Memory.
11. Of Fancy.
12. Of Natural Fools.
13. Of Recreations.
14. Of Tombs.

CHAP.
15. Of Deformities.
16. Of Plantations.
17. Of Contentment.
18. Of Books.
19. Of Time-serving.
20. Of Moderation.
21. Of Gravity.
22. Of Marriage.
23. Of Fame.
24. Of the Antiquity of Churches, and the necessity of them.
25. Of Ministers' maintenance.

These lives, characters, and moral Essays would, I think, fill two or three volumes in octavo, but they are written in so minute a character that I cannot form any conjecture to be depended upon. They are but a small part of the MS. works which Mr. Ferrar left behind him, which, as appears from some papers still existing, amounted to five volumes in folio. He was of opinion that instruction merely by precept might sometimes become dry and wearisome, and therefore was desirous to enliven his lectures by something that might give pleasure to the fancy at the same time that it conveyed wisdom to the heart. But he had great objection to plays, novels, and romances, and to poems, that were then and indeed have ever since been in great esteem. He thought that in many instances they did not tend to the important point which he had in view. But he reflected also that our SAVIOUR Himself frequently delivered His discourses in parables; and therefore that fable to a certain degree, might be admitted in moral instruction. With this view he composed those stories, and essays, which were intended to enliven their readings, and conversations. Besides these, he drew up regular discourses upon all the fasts, and feasts of the Church, and these also in their order made part of the readings. Every one of the young people, from the eldest to the youngest, male and female, was exercised every day in these public readings, and repetitions: by which the memory was wonderfully strengthened, and they all attained great excellence in speaking with propriety and grace.

But now four of Mr. Collet's eldest daughters

being grown up to woman's estate, to perfect them in the practice of good housewifery, Mr. Ferrar appointed them in rotation to take the whole charge of the domestic economy. Each had this care for a month, when her accounts were regularly passed, allowed, and delivered over to the next in succession. There was also the same care and regularity required with respect to the surgeon's chest: and the due provision of medicines and all things necessary for those who were sick, or hurt by any misfortune. A convenient apartment was provided for those of the family who chanced to be indisposed, called the infirmary, where they might be attended, and properly taken care of, without disturbance from any part of the numerous family. A large room was also set apart for the reception of the medicines, and of those who were brought in sick, or hurt, and wanted immediate assistance. The young ladies were required to dress the wounds of those who were hurt, in order to give them readiness and skill in this employment, and to habituate them to the virtues of humility, and tenderness of heart. The office relative to pharmacy, the weekly inspection, the prescription, and administration of medicines, Mr. Ferrar reserved to himself, being an excellent physician; as he had for many years attentively studied the theory and practice of medicine, both when Physic Fellow at Clare Hall, and under the celebrated professors at Padua. In this way was a considerable part of their income disposed of, and thus did Mr. Ferrar form his nieces to be wise and useful, virtuous, and valuable women.

In order to give some variety to this system of education, he formed the family into a sort of collegiate institution, of which one was considered as the founder, another guardian, a third as moderator, and himself as visitor of this little academy. The seven virgin daughters formed the junior part of this Society, were called the Sisters, and assumed the names of 1st. The Chief. 2nd. The Patient. 3rd. The Cheerful. 4th. The Affectionate. 5th. The Submiss. 6th. The Obedient. 7th. The Moderate. These all had their respective characters to sustain, and exercises to perform suited to those characters.

For the Christmas season of the year 1631, he composed twelve excellent discourses, five suited to the festivals within the twelve days, and seven to the assumed name and character of the Sisters. These were enlivened by hymns and odes composed by Mr. Ferrar, and set to music by the musicmaster of the family, who accompanied the voices with a viol, or the lute. That exercise which was to be performed by the Patient, is alone to be ex-

L

cepted. There was not any poetry, or music at the opening of this as of all the rest: the discourse itself was of a very serious turn, it was much longer than any other, and had not any historical anecdote, or fable interwoven into the body of it. The contrivance here was to exercise that virtue which it was intended to teach.

Amongst other articles of instruction and amusement Mr. Ferrar entertained an ingenious bookbinder who taught the family, females as well as males, the whole art and skill of bookbinding, gilding, lettering, and what they called pasting-printing, by the use of the rolling-press. By this assistance he composed a full harmony, or concordance of the four Evangelists, adorned with many beautiful pictures, which required more than a year for the composition, and was divided into 150 heads or chapters. For this purpose he set apart a handsome room near the Oratory. Here he had a large table, two printed copies of the Evangelists, of the same edition, and great store of the best and strongest white paper. Here he spent more than an hour every day in the contrivance of this book, and in directing his nieces, who attended him for that purpose, how they should cut out such and such particular passages out of the two printed copies of any part of each Evangelist, and then lay them together so as to perfect such a head or chapter as he had designed. This they did first roughly, and then with nice knives and scissors so neatly fitted each passage to the next belonging to it, and afterwards pasted them so evenly and smoothly together, upon large sheets of the best white paper, by the help of the rolling press, that many curious persons who saw the work when it was done, were deceived, and thought that it had been printed in the ordinary way. This was the *mechanical method* which he followed in compiling his Harmony. The title of his book was as follows. "The actions, doctrines, and other passages touching our Blessed LORD and SAVIOUR JESUS CHRIST, as they are related in the four Evangelists, reduced into one complete body of history: wherein that which is severally related by them is digested into order; and that which is jointly related by all or any of them is, first, expressed in their own words by way of comparison; secondly, brought into one narration by way of composition; thirdly, extracted into one clear context by way of collection; yet so as whatsoever was omitted in the context is inserted by way of supplement in another print, and in such a manner as all the four Evangelists may be easily read severally and distinctly; each apart and alone from first to last: and in each page throughout the book are sundry pictures added, expressing either the facts themselves, or their types and figures; or other things appertaining thereunto. The whole divided into 150 heads."

Several of the harmonies[1] were afterwards finished upon the same plan with some improvements: one of these books was presented to Mr. Ferrar's most dear and intimate friend, the well known Mr. Geo. Herbert, who in his letter of thanks for it, calls it a most inestimable jewel: another was given to his other singular friend Dr. Jackson. The fame of this work, the production of a man so celebrated as the author had been, soon reached the ears of the king (Charles I.,) who took the first opportunity to make himself personally acquainted with it, by obtaining the perusal of it.

Mr. Ferrar about this time wrote several very valuable treatises, and made several translations from authors in different languages, on subjects which he thought might prove serviceable to the cause of religion. Among others, having long had a high opinion of John Valdesso's *Hundred and ten Considerations*, &c., a book which he met with in

[1] The book in S. John's College library at Oxford (said to be compiled by the Nuns of Gidding) is one of these Harmonies, being all patch-work.

his travels, he now, (in 1632) translated it from the Italian copy into English, and sent it to be examined and censured by his friend Mr. Herbert before it was made public: which excellent book Mr. Herbert returned with many marginal notes, and criticisms, as they are now printed with it; with an affectionate letter also recommending the publication.

In May, 1633, his Majesty set out upon his journey to Scotland, and in his progress he stepped a little out of his road to view Little Gidding in Huntingdonshire. The family having notice, met his Majesty at the extremity of the parish, at a place called, from this event, the King's Close: and in the form of their solemn processions conducted him to their church, which he viewed with great pleasure. He inquired into, and was informed of the particulars of their public, and domestic economy: but it does not appear that at this time he made any considerable stay. The following summer his Majesty and the Queen passed two nights at Apethorp in Northamptonshire, the seat of Mildmay Fane, Earl of Westmoreland. From thence he sent one of his gentlemen to *intreat* (his Majesty's own word) a sight of *the Concordance*, which, he had heard, was some time since done at

Gidding; with assurance that in a few days, when he had perused it, he would send it back again. Mr. N. Ferrar was then in London, and the family made some little demur, not thinking it worthy to be put into his Majesty's hands; but at length they delivered it to the messenger. But it was not returned in a few days, or weeks: some months were elapsed, when the gentleman brought it back from the King, who was then at London. He said he had many things to deliver to the family from his master. First, to yield the King's hearty thanks to them all for the sight of the book, which passed the report he had heard of it. Then to signify his approbation of it, in all respects. Next to excuse him in two points. The first for not returning it as soon as he had promised: the other, for that he had in many places of the margin written notes in it with his own hand. " And (which I know will please you,") said the gentleman, "you will find an instance of my master's humility in one of the margins. The place I mean is where he had written something with his own hand, and then put it out again, acknowledging that he was mistaken in that particular."

The gentleman farther told them, that the King took such delight in it, that he passed some part of

NICOLAS FERRAR. 115

every day in perusing it. And lastly, he said, to show you how true this is, and that what I have declared is no court compliment, I am expressly commanded by my master, earnestly to request of you, Mr. Nicolas Ferrar, and of the young ladies, that you would make him one of these books for his own use, and if you will please to undertake it, his Majesty says you will do him a most acceptable service."

Mr. Nicolas Ferrar and the young ladies returned their most humble duty, and immediately set about what the King desired. In about a year's time it was finished, and it was sent to London to be presented to his Majesty by Dr. Laud, then made Archbishop of Canterbury, and Dr. Cosin, Master of Peterhouse, whose turn it was to wait that month, being one of the King's Chaplains. This book was bound entirely by Mary Collet (one of Mr. Ferrar's nieces) all wrought in gold, in a new and most elegant fashion.

The King after long and serious looking it over, said, "This is indeed a most valuable work, and in many respects worthy to be presented to the greatest Prince upon earth. For the matter it contains is the richest of all treasures. The laborious composure of it into this excellent form of a Harmony, the judicious contrivance of the method, the curious workmanship in so neatly cutting out and disposing the text, the nice laying of these costly pictures, and the exquisite art expressed in the binding, are, I really think, not to be equalled. I must acknowledge myself to be indeed greatly indebted to the family for this jewel: and whatever is in my power, I shall at any time be ready to do for any of them."

Then after some pause, taking the book into his hands, he said, "And what think you, my lord of Canterbury, and you, Dr. Cosin, if I should ask a second favour of these good people? indeed I have another request to make to them, and it is this. I often read over the lives and actions of the Kings of Judah and Israel in the books of the Kings, and the Chronicles, and I frequently meet with difficulties. I should be much obliged if Mr. Ferrar would make me such a book as may bring all these matters together into one regular narration, that I may read the whole in one continued story and yet at the same time may be able to see them separate; or what belongs to one book, and what to another. I have long ago moved several of my chaplains to undertake this business: but it is not done: I suppose it is attended with too much difficulty. Will you, my lord, apply for me to

Mr. Ferrar?" The Archbishop wrote to Mr. Ferrar, acquainting him with the King's desires, and Mr. Ferrar immediately set himself about the work.

In the course of little more than a year, about Oct. 1636, Mr. Ferrar and his assistants completed the Harmony of the two books of the Kings and the Chronicles, and young Nicolas Ferrar bound it in purple velvet, most richly gilt. It was then sent to the Archbishop and Dr. Cosin, to be by them presented to the King. His Majesty was extremely delighted with it, saying, " It was a fit mirror for a King's daily inspection. Herein," he said, " I shall behold GOD's mercies and judgments: His punishing of evil princes, and rewarding the good. To these His promises, to those His threatenings most surely accomplished. I have a second time gained a great treasure. What I said of the first book, I may most justly say of this; and I desire you will let them know my high esteem both of it and of them." Dr. Cosin then presented a letter from Mr. Ferrar, which the King declared he thought the finest composition he ever read. In farther discoursing of these Harmonies with the Divines, the King determined that for public benefit they should be printed under his own immediate command and protection. But the troubles of the ensuing times prevented this laudable purpose from being carried into execution. The title of this second Harmony was as follows:

"The History of the Israelites, from the death of King Saul, to their carrying away captive into Babylon: collected out of the books of the Kings, and Chronicles, in the words of the text, without any alteration of importance by addition to or diminution from them. Whereby, first, all the actions and passages related in any of the books of the Kings and Chronicles, whether jointly or severally, are reduced into the body of one complete narration. Secondly, they are digested into an orderly dependence one upon the other. Thirdly, many difficult places are cleared, and many seeming differences between the books of Kings and Chronicles compounded. And this is so contrived, as, notwithstanding the mutual compositions of the books into one historical collection, yet the form of each of them is preserved entire, in such a manner as they may be easily read, severally and distinctly from first to last. Together with several tables. The first summarily declaring the several heads or chapters into which the historical collection is divided. The second specifying what passages are related *severally* in the aforesaid books, and what are *jointly* related by them both: as also in what heads and chapters in this collection they may be found. The third, showing where every chapter of the texts themselves, and every part of them may be readily found in this historical collection."

These are probably the last works of this sort, executed by Mr. Ferrar, who died in little more than a year, and was very weak and infirm a considerable time before his death. But the connection between the King and this family did not cease on Mr. Ferrar's death. For it appears from several papers still in being, that there was what may be justly called a friendly intercourse subsisting, even till the distressful year 1646.

In fitting up the house at Gidding, moral sentences, and short passages from the Scriptures had been put up in various places; and in the great parlour was an inscription which gave rise to much speculation and censure. It was nevertheless first approved of by several judicious Divines, and particularly by Mr. Herbert, who advised it to be engraved in brass, and so hung up that it might be seen of all. But calumny was now gone forth, and nothing could be done at Gidding that was not subjected to the severest misrepresentation. The inscription was as follows.

IHS

He who (by reproof of our errors, and remonstrance of that which is more perfect) seeks to make us better, is welcome as an angel of GOD.	And	He who (by a cheerful participation of that which is good) confirms us in the same, is welcome as a Christian Friend.

But

He who any ways goes about to disturb us in that which is and ought to be amongst Christians (though it be not usual in the world) is a burden whilst he stays and shall bear his judgment whosoever he be.	And	He who faults us in absence for that which in presence he made show to approve of, doth by a double guilt of flattery and slander violate the bands both of friendship and charity.

Mary Ferrar, Widow,
Mother of this Family,
aged fourscore years,
(who bids adieu to all fears and hopes of this world
and only desires to serve GOD)
set up this Table.

The extraordinary course of life pursued at Gidding, the strictness of their rules, their prayers, literally without ceasing, their abstinence, mortifications, nightly watchings, and various other peculiarities, gave birth to censure in some, and inflamed the malevolence of others, but excited the wonder and curiosity of all. So that they were frequently visited with different views by persons of all denominations, and of opposite opinions. They received all who came with courteous civility; and from those who were inquisitive they concealed nothing: for in truth there was not anything either in their opinions or their practice that was in the least degree necessary to be concealed. They were at the time, notwithstanding all the real good they did, severally slandered and vilified: by some they were abused as Papists: by others as Puritans. Mr. Ferrar himself, though possessed of uncommon patience, and resignation, yet in anguish of spirit complained to his friends, that the perpetual obloquy he endured was a sort of unceasing martyrdom.

These clamorous abuses were spread about with great virulence and malignity. But no one, who is acquainted with the spirit of those times, and considers to what a degree Religious rancour had possessed the hearts of all men—how intolerant the Puritans were of the Papists, and of the Church of England—what detestation the Papists had of the Church of England, and of the Puritans—and what a shameful persecution the governors of the established Church exercised, often against the Papists, and always against the Protestant Dissenters—will wonder that a society of devotees, who were apprehended not to agree with any of them, should be persecuted by them all.

Hence violent invectives, and inflammatory pamphlets were published against them. Amongst others, not long after Mr. Ferrar's death, a Treatise was addressed to the Parliament, entitled, *The Arminian Nunnery*, or a brief description and relation of the late erected Monastical Place, called the Arminian Nunnery at Little Gidding in Huntingdonshire: humbly addressed to the wise consideration of the present Parliament. The foundation is by a company of Ferrars at Gidding. Printed for Thomas Underhill, 1641.

In this production there is nothing but falsehood, or what is much worse, truth wilfully so mangled and misrepresented as to answer the vilest ends of falsehood. And this sort of malignity was carried to such a length, that not long before the real tragedy of King Charles was perpetrated, certain soldiers of the Parliament party resolved to plunder the house at Gidding. The family being informed of their hasty approach, thought it prudent to fly, and, as to their persons, endeavour to escape the intended violence.

These military zealots, in the rage of what they called reformation, ransacked both the church and the house. In doing which they expressed a particular spite against the organ. This they broke in pieces, of which they made a large fire, and thereat roasted several of Mr. Ferrar's sheep, which they had killed in his grounds. This done, they seized all the plate, furniture, and provision which they could conveniently carry away. And in this general devastation perished those works of Mr. Nicolas Ferrar which merited a better fate.

Certainly no family suffered more from less cause of offence: for though they were pious and firm members of the Church of England, they behaved themselves quietly and with Christian benevolence towards all men of all denominations: and although they practised austerities which were not exceeded by the severest orders of the Monastic institutions, yet they neither required them from others, nor in themselves attributed any saving merit to them.

A short time before the commission of these violences, Bishop Williams paid his last friendly visit at Gidding, and seeing the inscription in the parlour said to Mr. John Ferrar, "I would advise you to take this table down. You see the times grow high and turbulent, and no one knows where the rage and madness of the people may end. I am just come from Boston, where I was used very coarsely. I do not speak as by authority, I only advise you as a friend, for fear of offence or worse consequences." Then after sincerely condoling with them on their irreparable misfortune in the death of Nicolas Ferrar, he bade them his final farewell: but ever after continued their firm friend, and constantly vindicated the family from the many slanders of their false accusers.—But to return from this digression.

Mrs. Ferrar, towards the close of her life, seems to have been convinced that the mortifications practised by the family, were more than were necessary, and she became apprehensive for the health, and even for the life of her beloved son. She therefore earnestly entreated him, and with many tears besought him, that he would relax a little in the severe discipline which he exercised upon himself. And he, being an example of filial obedience, complied in some degree with her request, during the remainder of her life: but this was not of long continuance.

In the year 1635, ten years after coming to Gidding, this excellent woman died, aged eighty-three years. Her character, as follows, is given by her son Mr. John Ferrar, who collected, and left the materials for these memoirs. "Though of so great age, at her dying day, she had no infirmity, and scarce any sign of old age upon her. Her hearing, sight, and all her senses were very good. She had never lost a tooth; she walked very upright, and with great agility. Nor was she troubled with any pains or uneasiness of body. While she lived at Gidding she rose, summer and winter, at five o'clock, and sometimes sooner. In her person she was of a comely presence, and had a countenance so full of gravity that it drew respect from all who beheld her. In her words she was courteous, in her actions obliging. In her diet always very temperate; saying, she did not live to eat and drink, but ate and drank to live. She was a pattern of piety, benevolence, and charity. And thus she lived and died, esteemed, revered, and beloved of all who knew her." Such are the effects of a life of temperance and virtue.

While his mother was yet living Mr. Ferrar did so far comply with her request, that he went to bed, or lay down upon it, from nine in the evening till one in the morning, which was his constant hour of rising to his devotions. But after her death he never did either: but wrapping himself in a loose frieze gown, slept on a bear's skin upon the boards. He also watched either in the Oratory, or in the Church three nights in the week.

These nightly watchings having been frequently mentioned, it may not be improper here to give a short account of the rules under which they were performed. It was agreed that there should be a constant double nightwatch, of men at one end of the house, and of women at the other. That each watch should consist of two or more persons. That the watchings should begin at nine o'clock at night and end at one in the morning. That each watch should in those four hours, carefully and distinctly say over the whole book of Psalms, in the way of antiphony, one repeating one verse, and the rest the other. That they should then pray for the life of the King and his sons. The time of their watch being ended, they went to Mr. Ferrar's door, bade him good morrow, and left a lighted candle for him. At one he constantly rose, and betook himself to religious meditation, founding this practice on a literal acceptation of the passage, "At midnight will I rise and give thanks," and some other passages of similar import. Several religious persons both in the neighbourhood, and from distant places, attended these watchings: and amongst these the celebrated Mr. Richard Crashaw, Fellow of Peterhouse, who was very intimate in the family and frequently came from Cambridge for this purpose, and at his return often watched in Little S. Mary's Church, near Peterhouse.[1]

[1] A most respectable author has given his sanction, if not to the severity, at least to a moderate observation of this mode of Psalmody, in his comment on the 134th Psalm.

"Bless ye the LORD, all ye servants of the LORD, who *by night* stand in the house of the LORD. Bless Him in the cheerful and busy hours of the day: bless Him in the solemn and peaceful *watches* of the night.

"The pious Mr. Nicolas Ferrar exhibited in the last

His friends perceiving a visible decay of his strength, remonstrated against these austerities, fearing bad consequences to his health; they told him that he was much too strict in his way of life; they advised him to go abroad, to take the air frequently, and to admit of some innocent amusement. He replied, that to rise and go to bed when we please, to take the air and get a good appetite, to eat heartily, to drink wine, and cheer the spirits, to hunt, and hawk, to ride abroad, and make visits, to play at cards and dice, these are what the world terms gallant and pleasant things, and recreations fit for a gentleman : but such a life would be so great a slavery to me, and withal I think it of so dangerous a tendency, that if I was told I must either live in that manner, or presently suffer death, the latter would most certainly be my choice.

About three months before his death, perceiving in himself some inward faintness, and apprehending that his last hour was now drawing very near, he broke off abruptly from writing any farther on a

century an instance of a Protestant family, in which a constant course of Psalmody was appointed, and so strictly kept up, that through the whole four and twenty hours of day and night, there was no portion of time when some of the members were not employed in performing that most pleasant part of duty and devotion."
—Dr. Horne.

subject which was then under his consideration. This breaking off is yet to be seen in that unfinished treatise, with his reason for discontinuing it. He then began to write down *Contemplations on Death* in the following words.

"The remembrance of death is very powerful to restrain us from sinning. For he who shall well consider that the day will come (and he knoweth not how soon) when he shall be laid on a sick bed, weak and faint, without ease and almost without strength, encompassed with melancholy thoughts, and overwhelmed with anguish; when on one side, his distemper increasing upon him, the physician tells him that he is past all hope of life, and on the other, his friends urge him to dispose of his worldly goods, and share his wealth among them: that wealth which he procured with trouble, and preserved with anxiety: that wealth which he now parts from with sorrow: when again the Priest calls on him to take the preparatory measures for his departure: when he himself now begins to be assured that here he hath no abiding city; that this is no longer a world for him: that no more suns will rise and set upon him: that for him there will be no more seeing, no more hearing, no more speaking, no more touching, no more tasting, no more fancying, no more understanding, no more remembering, no more desiring, no more loving, no more delights of any sort to be enjoyed by him; but that death will at one stroke deprive him of all these things: that he will speedily be carried out of the house which he had called his own, and is now become another's: that he will be put into a cold, narrow grave: that earth will be consigned to earth, ashes to ashes, and dust to dust: let any man duly and daily ponder these things, and how can it be that he should dare"——

Here the strength of this good man failed him, and his essay is left thus unfinished.

On the second of November he found that his weakness increased, yet he went to church, and on that day officiated for the last time. After this, his faintness continued gradually to increase, but he suffered not the least degree of bodily pain. He conversed with his family and earnestly encouraged them to persevere in the way he had pointed out to them. And addressing himself particularly to his brother, said, "My dear brother, I must now shortly appear before GOD, and give an account of what I have taught this family. And here with a safe conscience I can say, that I have delivered nothing to you but what I thought agreeable to His word: therefore abide steadily by what I have taught. Worship GOD in spirit and in truth. I will use no more words. One thing however I must add, that you may be both forewarned, and prepared. Sad times are coming on, very sad times indeed; you will live to see them." Then grasping his brother's hand, he said, "O! my brother! I pity you, who must see these dreadful alterations. And when you shall see the true worship of GOD brought to nought, and suppressed, then look, and fear that desolation is nigh at hand. And in this great trial may GOD of His infinite mercy support and deliver you."

The third day before his death he summoned all his family round him, and then desired his brother to go and mark out a place for his grave according to the particular directions he then gave. When his brother returned, saying it was done as he desired, he requested them all in presence of each other to take out of his study three large hampers full of books, which had been there locked up many years. "They are comedies, tragedies, heroic Poems, and romances; let them be immediately burnt upon the place marked out for my grave; and when you shall have so done, come back and inform me." When information was brought him that they were all consumed, he desired that this act might be considered as the testimony of his disapprobation of all such productions, as tending to corrupt the mind of man, and improper for the perusal of every good and sincere Christian.

On the first of December, 1637, he found himself declining very fast, and desired to receive the Sacrament: after which, and taking a most affectionate farewell of all his family, without a struggle, or a groan, he expired in a rapturous ecstasy of devotion.

Thus lived, and thus died Nicolas Ferrar, the best of sons, of brothers, and of friends, on Monday, December, 2, 1637, precisely as the clock struck one: the hour at which for many years he constantly rose to pay his addresses to heaven.

That he was eminently pious towards GOD, benevolent towards man, and perfectly sincere in all his dealings; that he was industrious beyond his strength, and indefatigable in what he thought his duty; that he was blessed by Providence with uncommon abilities, and by unremitted exertion of his various talents attained many valuable accomplishments, is very manifest from the preceding memoirs, and is the least that can be said in his praise: and though greatly to his honour, is yet no more than that degree of excellence which may have been attained by many. But the spiritual exaltation of mind by which he rose above all earthly considerations of advantage, and devoted himself entirely to

GOD, Whom in the strictest sense he loved with all his heart, with all his soul, and with all his strength, being united to the active virtues of a citizen of the world, gives him a peculiar pre-eminence even among those who excel in virtue. For while he practised self-denial to the utmost, and exercised religious severities upon himself scarce inferior to those of the recluses who retired to deserts, and shut themselves up in dens and caves of the earth, yet he did not, like them, by a solitary and morose retirement, deprive himself of the power continually to do good, but led a life of active virtue and benevolence. His youth was spent in an incessant application to learned studies, and the time of his travel was given to the acquisition of universal wisdom. On his return home, in conducting the affairs of an important establishment, he displayed uncommon abilities, integrity and spirit. As a member of the House of Commons he gained distinguished honour, and was appointed the principal manager to prosecute, and bring to justice the great man, and corrupt Minister of that time. And having thus discharged the duties of a virtuous citizen, he devoted the rest of his life to the instruction of youth, to works of Christian charity, and to the worship of GOD in a religious retirement, while he was yet in possession of his health and strength, and in the prime of manhood; that like the great author, who was his daily and nightly study and admiration, the royal Psalmist, he might not sacrifice to GOD, that which cost him nothing. In one word, he was a rare example of that excellence in which are blended all the brilliant qualities of the great man, with all the amiable virtues of the good.

If by the brightness of his example he may have given such light to any who sat in darkness and the shadow of death, as to guide their feet into the ways of peace, he has not lived in vain, nor been an useless burthen upon the earth.

"He gave his mind to the law of the Most High, and was occupied in the meditation thereof. He gave his heart to resort *early* to the LORD who made him, and prayed before Him. He was filled with the spirit of understanding, he poured out wise sentences, and gave thanks unto the LORD. Many shall commend his understanding, and so long as the world endureth it shall not be blotted out: his memorial shall not depart away, and his name shall live from generation to generation." Ecclus. xxxix.

J. MASTERS and SON, Albion Buildings, Bartholomew Close, E.C.

www.ingramcontent.com/pod-product-compliance
Lightning Source LLC
Chambersburg PA
CBHW031323160426
43196CB00007B/645